THE **FOOD DOCTOR** DIET

THE FOOD DOCTOR DIET

Ian Marber, MBANT, Dip ION

For more information
from The Food Doctor visit
www.thefooddoctor.com

DK PUBLISHING

London, New York, Munich, Melbourne, Delhi

For my father, with love and heartfelt admiration

Project editor	Susannah Steel
Designer	Mark Cavanagh
Managing editor	Stephanie Farrow
DTP designer	Sonia Charbonnier
Production controller	Stuart Masheter
Art director	Carole Ash
Category publisher	Mary-Clare Jerram
Food stylist/home economist	Pippin Britz
Photographer	Sian Irvine
US Editor	Barbara Berger
US Nutrition Consultant	Lisa Mandelbaum, MS, RD CDN, Joy Bauer Nutrition
US Copyeditor	Laaren Brown
US Editorial Assistant	John Searcy

Note to readers:
Do not attempt the Seven-day Diet if you are pregnant or under 18. Please consult your doctor first if you have a diagnosed medical condition.

First American Edition, 2003
2 4 6 8 10 9 7 5 3

Published in the United States
by DK Publishing, Inc.
375 Hudson Street
New York, New York 10014

DK Publishing, Inc. offers special discounts for bulk purchases for sales promotions or premiums. Specific, large-quantity needs can be met with special editions, including personalized covers, excerpts of existing guides, and corporate imprints. For more information, contact: Special Markets Department, DK Publishing, Inc., 375 Hudson Street, New York, NY 10014 Fax: 212-689-5254

　　　Library of Congress Cataloging-in-Publication Data
Marber, Ian.
　The food doctor diet : a simple plan for life-long healthy eating and
natural weight control / Ian Marber.
　　p. cm.
Includes index.
　ISBN 0-7894-9692-5 (alk. paper)
　1. Nutrition. 2. Food. 3. Health. 4. Diet. I. Title.
RA784.M296 2004
613.2--dc22
　　　　　　　　　　2003055486

ISBN 0-7894-9692-5

Color reproduction by Colourscan, Singapore
Printed and bound in Germany by Mohndruck GmbH

Discover more at
www.dk.com

Contents

Introduction

My career as a nutritionist has encompassed everything from giving individual consultations and workshops to writing newspaper columns and magazine articles and appearing on television and radio. And yet I know that the first question people will always ask me is, "How can I lose weight?"

Before you think that I have inherited a gene that helps me stay trim, and that I don't know how it feels to be frustrated and uncomfortable about weight issues, you should know that I have battled with my own weight over the years. There have been times when I have felt immense pressure to diet since, given my profession, I am supposed to be slim. It has taken me some time to work out how to maintain a comfortable weight, and I am sure that I could lose a few more pounds. Nevertheless, I have come to terms with the fact that the weight I want to be, or feel I should be, isn't always a realistic goal.

The dieting cycle

I have been asked to write diet books before, but I shied away because I didn't want to jump on any bandwagons. However, having worked with so many clients who have followed fad diets, "quick fixes," and potentially unsafe weight-loss programs, I feel that now is the right time to debunk the myths and help people achieve their goals.

Let me start with some semantics. Our understanding of the word "diet" is as a short-term eating program with a beginning, a middle, and an end. You follow the regimen, lose weight, then revert to your old eating habits and so gain weight. You blame the diet—"It didn't work for me"—buy another book or join another club, and off you go again. You gain the weight back—and maybe more—in the interim, of course, and then turn to another diet, hoping that this one will work for you. There is one winner and one loser in this cycle: you lose money and self-esteem, while the diet industry gains another long-term customer.

I have read nearly every diet book there is, and while many diets have some really good elements to them, they can be pretty hard to understand without a degree in biochemistry, and many are difficult to follow unless you don't mind endlessly weighing food. But that's not the worst of it. Some diet experts suggest eating only particular foods, or insist that their program will fail unless you eat hard-to-find foods or prepacked meals exclusively. It is no wonder that so many people fail to lose weight.

What's different about this diet?

The Food Doctor weight-loss plan focuses primarily on achieving good health, especially that of the digestive system. I believe that if you follow my plan, and also make good digestive health your main aim, you should succeed in your goal to lose weight and feel great.

I also believe that if you understand just how good health can be achieved, you will be able to apply the plan to your own lifestyle, taking into account your income, working hours, commitments, and social life.

I believe that if you follow my plan, and also make **good digestive health** your **main aim,** you should **succeed** in your goal to **lose weight** and feel **great**

Digestion—a quick tour

I believe that a healthy digestive system enhances the absorption of nutrients, and can go a long way towards reducing cravings for sugary, processed foods and drinks. So let me first explain briefly about the process of digestion. By the way, turn to the glossary (see pp.138–39) if you are unsure of any terms or words.

Digestion is the process of breaking down food for the body to absorb. As we eat, the combination of enzymes in our saliva and the process of chewing start to break down our food. However, saliva is relatively mild and is

> Lesson number one is to **chew** your food **properly** so that your body can **digest** it **effectively**

limited in its effectiveness, so you must chew well. If you don't chew your food, you are at a disadvantage, the consequences of which are explained in more detail below. If you do chew each mouthful properly, your body can begin to digest it more effectively.

The digestive tract is a series of connected organs. Once you have swallowed your food, it passes on down the osphagus to the stomach (which is located under the rib cage and not at the navel, as many people seem to think). Here it is churned many times with a variety of substances, most notably with hydrochloric acid, which is a potent acid that further breaks food. Yet, however strong hydrochloric acid is, if you haven't chewed your food properly, it probably won't be broken down as well as it could while in the stomach.

At the end of this stage, which can take several hours, the partly-digested food is known as chyme, an acid pulp that is released through a valve into the intestines. It is in the intestines that the nutrients are filtered out and absorbed into the bloodstream: the chyme is constantly turned over and passed back and forth in each area of intestine so that it is exposed to tiny little intestinal protrusions called villi, which filter out the nutrients. The chyme continues along the intestines as if on a conveyor belt until all the nutrients

have been taken out and only waste is left, which is then released from the body as feces.

I believe that digestive problems occur if the efficient workings of the digestive system are impaired by the sort of diet and lifestyle that have probably been largely responsible for excess weight in the first place. A diet that is high in refined sugars and saturated fats, combined with lack of chewing and high stress levels, can create an internal environment in which foods are not broken down properly and nutrients are poorly absorbed. Our energy levels can also soar and dip sharply in response to a high intake of refined sugars, which can lead to sugar cravings that we interpret as hunger—and so the cycle continues.

Bacteria balance

Inside the intestines are countless bacteria that also have a profound effect on your digestive health. Some bacteria, called *Lactobacillus acidophilus* and *Lactobacillus bifidum bacterium*, are beneficial to the intestines, some are innocuous and others, in large amounts, can be defined as potentially unfriendly bacteria, such as the *Citrobacter freundii, Klebsiella pneumoniae,* and *Bacillus* species. So the right balance of bacteria is crucial to your digestive health. A stool analysis, which can be arranged by your doctor or nutrition consultant, will reveal just how well your digestive system is working.

Checking your internal health

You can get a clue to your internal health just by looking at your tongue in a mirror: I have noticed that the majority of my clients with digestive problems have a white or slightly green coating on their tongue. Even if you don't see a coating, if your diet is high in saturated fats, processed food or sugar, your intestines may not be as healthy as you would like them to be.

As we chew, enzymes i the process of breaking

our saliva help in
down our food

Fingernails that are hard and that do not flake are usually a sign of good digestive health

Another sign that all is not as well as it could be internally is a slight swelling or protrusion just below where the sternum ends. This could be a sign of bloating. In fact, bloating is by far the most frequent complaint that I have seen in clients in recent years. Other clues include flatulence, alternating diarrhea and constipation, and/or bad breath. Furthermore, some of my clients who have flaky or soft fingernails that break easily will often notice an improvement in the quality of their nails after appropriate changes have been made to their diet.

Hidden dangers

Beneficial bacteria are now contained in many sweetened yogurts and drinks, but unless you eat or drink these products in large amounts they can be limited in the extent to which they improve the levels of friendly bacteria in your system.

Many products that are marketed as healthy are, in fact, loaded with sugar. This ingredient helps make the drink palatable and, since bacteria feed on sugar, it ensures that they survive the packaging and storage process. The problem is that both friendly and unfriendly bacteria feed on the sugar once it is in the intestines. So the health effects of these drinks or yogurts can be limited, given their high sugar content.

Not only does sugar encourage the proliferation of unfriendly bacteria, I feel that a diet high in sugary foods can lead to weight gain and food cravings. If you exclude refined sugars from your diet, you can improve your digestive health and reduce any cravings for sugar.

You should be aware that low-fat foods are also often loaded with sugar in some form. A low-fat or calorie-controlled diet is therefore automatically higher in refined sugars than a diet that I believe is best for good intestinal health.

High levels of yeasts

The intestines also contain yeasts that can affect digestion. The best known is *Candida albicans,* which can cause symptoms such as oral yeast infections, fatigue, and sugar and alcohol cravings. Yeasts, in moderation, have a positive role to play in the intestines, but it is thought that they may proliferate if your diet is high in sugar, alcohol, and saturated fats.

Gut inflammation

High levels of unfriendly bacteria and yeasts and low levels of friendly bacteria can cause the intestinal lining to become inflamed. This sensitive barrier is as thin as the skin on the eyelids, so it's easy to see how vulnerable it can be. If it does become inflamed, I believe tiny food particles may pass through it, attracting the attention of the immune system, which then sends out specific cells to deal with these unwanted substances—the next time you eat the same food, your immune system may react to it. I consider this to be how a food intolerance is born: if your gut is not healthy and intact, today's meal can become tomorrow's problem.

Parasite problems

Parasites are the last part of the story. Transmitted through the skin in contaminated food or water, they can cause severe digestive problems. The most common parasite is *Blastocystis hominis.* If you suspect that you have a parasite or a bacterial problem, ask a doctor or nutrition consultant for a stool analysis and advice about appropriate treatment, especially if you are pregnant or nursing.

So, by encouraging beneficial bacteria to proliferate in the gut, and by reducing its levels of unfriendly bacteria, sugar, yeasts, and any possible parasites, you can greatly improve your chances of good overall digestive health.

Eating **healthfully** encourages **beneficial bacteria** to **proliferate** and **reduces** levels of potentially **unfriendly bacteria**, yeasts and any possible parasites

Complex and simple carbohydrates

So just what should you eat to encourage good digestive health? Foods known as carbohydrates are broken down by the body into glucose, the fuel that cells use to make energy. That's the energy necessary for every function, from breathing and thinking to moving and digesting. Carbohydrates that are low in fiber are broken down quickly into glucose to supply a surge of energy. However, your energy levels soon fall just as quickly, leaving you hungry so that you eat more food and gain weight. In contrast, carbohydrates that are high in fibre are broken down more slowly by the body. So, by eating high-fiber carbohydrates in the correct amounts, I believe that you will achieve successful weight loss.

The best way to think of food being broken down by the body is to compare, for example, a raw carrot to a glass of carrot juice. You must chew the carrot well as it's a fibrous vegetable, and it is this fiber content that slows the rate at which the carrot is digested. This slow conversion time ensures that the levels of glucose in the blood rise gently, so the carrot is classified as a complex carbohydrate. The fiber in the carrot has other benefits, too: It helps lower cholesterol, maintains the right levels of gut bacteria, and is essential for a healthy cardio-vascular system. The list is almost endless.

If you take the same carrot and juice it, the nutrients may now be easier to absorb, but as the fiber has been removed, the juice is broken down quickly into glucose. Despite the fact that it is rich in nutrients, the juice is effectively now a refined, or simple, carbohydrate.

Insulin production

Glucose levels in the blood fluctuate all the time. If levels are high and surplus to immediate requirements—that is, if glucose is not being used to create energy—the body senses this and stimulates the pancreas to release insulin. This hormone encourages the body, through a series of biochemical changes, to store excess glucose in the muscles and liver to be used later. Once these stores are full, glucose is stored as fat. So a diet of foods that are broken down into glucose quickly will stimulate insulin production, and so add to your fat stores if you do not burn them off. If your diet only includes foods that take time to be broken down, and if you avoid large meals, your insulin levels will be kept to a minimum, allowing any fat stores to decrease.

The Food Doctor plan

By now you should have a good idea of what the Food Doctor plan is all about. In short, you will eat mainly lean proteins, essential fats, fiber, and some carbohydrates, but only those that are broken down slowly.

This book begins with a seven-day diet to improve your digestion and reduce fermentation in the gut. This is the toughest part of my plan, but don't let that put you off. It lasts only one week, and it forms the foundation for establishing good digestive health and losing weight.

The diet is followed by a long-term eating plan that shows you how to lose weight, slowly but surely, while benefiting from a diet rich in nutrients and fiber provided by the right balance of complex carbohydrates and proteins for good health. Remember that the success of any weight-loss plan is affected by your levels of physical activity. If you don't exercise, your chances of succeeding will be low. Following this plan with friends, family, or colleagues can make things easier and provide help and support when you need it. Above all, this plan is safe, sustainable, and simple. No science degree is required, little weighing of food is necessary, no food groups are excluded, and, best of all, there is room to cheat, too.

The way to think of food being **broken down** by the body is to compare a **raw carrot** to a glass of **carrot juice**

Juices and puréed soups are generally thought of as being healthy, but in my plan these foods are excluded unless they are drunk with a meal that contains protein and fiber to slow the digestion process. The high glucose levels generated by these simple carbohydrates stimulate insulin production, which can hinder weight loss.

Simple carbohydrates
have their fiber removed
and thus their inherent
form is changed

Seven -day diet

The Seven-Day Diet encourages good digestive health by reducing the amount of sugars and saturated fats you eat. Seven days is enough time for you to adapt to, and benefit from, the changes in your diet, yet short enough for you to achieve realistic goals. You will eat frequently, albeit in small amounts, so you shouldn't feel especially hungry. If there are certain foods that you can't eat, substitute one recipe for another recommended at a similar time of day, but try to stick to the suggested meals, as this balanced diet plan is carefully designed to promote health and well-being.

Preparing for the seven-day diet

Before you begin the Seven-Day Diet, keep a food diary of what you eat and drink over three days. This will help you identify which foods make up the bulk of your usual diet and will clarify the current state of your health *(see pp.20–21)*. During this time you can shop for the ingredients you will need for the week. It is also recommended that you talk to your doctor first, especially if you are very overweight or have other health problems.

Three-day diary

Before you begin the diet, the most important step is to keep a food diary. Photocopy this blank diary and fill it in as diligently as you can. Write down a list of everything you eat and drink, and at what time, over three consecutive days. There is also space to write down how you feel. This could include physical symptoms—for example, whether you feel lethargic or bloated—and even how you feel emotionally.

The changes in your eating habits over the next week will take some getting used to, so prepare for this by reminding yourself of the positive changes the Seven-Day Diet will make in your health. Write notes to yourself and post them in places where you keep food (cabinets, pantry, refrigerator, or desk drawer) so that you will be reminded to stay resolute and not waver while you are on the diet.

DAY ONE

Time	All meals, snacks, treats, and drinks

How do I feel?

DAY TWO

Time   All meals, snacks, treats, and drinks

How do I feel?

DAY THREE

Time   All meals, snacks, treats, and drinks

How I feel?

Shopping for the seven-day diet

Once you decide which day you'll begin the Seven-Day Diet *(see box, below)*, you can shop for most of the food you'll require before you start, leaving yourself just a few vegetables and some fresh fish to buy during the week. If you are well stocked with all the ingredients for the recipes, then the Seven-Day Diet will be much easier to follow, and you will also have no excuses for straying into stores and buying unsuitable alternatives at the last minute. Photocopy the lists on these pages and check off the ingredients as you shop for them. Buy organic food if you prefer, although the success of this diet does not depend on it.

DON'T START ON A MONDAY

How many times have you overdone things or veered from your eating plan over the weekend and then justified your actions by promising to start again on Monday? I know from experience that starting the Seven-Day Diet on a Monday makes the weekend seem a long way away. I recommend starting the diet on a Wednesday or Thursday so that if you need more sleep or if you experience any of the symptoms on pages 20–21, the weekend will be just around the corner, allowing you to take things easy. By the time Monday comes around, you will be feeling great, which will make it easier to tackle the challenges of the new week.

Shopping list for the Seven-Day Diet

Dried foods
- ☐ 1lb (450g) old-fashioned oats
- ☐ 1lb (450g) quinoa

- ☐ 1 package unsalted rice cakes
- ☐ 1 package melba toasts
- ☐ 1 package rye crispbreads

- ☐ 1 small package pumpkin seeds
- ☐ 1 small package sesame seeds
- ☐ 1 small package sunflower seeds
- ☐ 1 small package flaxseeds
- ☐ 1 small package pine nuts
- ☐ 1 small package cashew nuts
- ☐ 9oz (250g) raisins
- ☐ 2 small packages mixed raw nuts, including cashews, brazil nuts, almonds, walnuts, and hazelnuts

For the muesli mix
To make the Seven-Day Diet muesli mix, buy a small packet each of any **four** of the following grains:
- ☐ Barley flakes
- ☐ Rye flakes
- ☐ Oat flakes
- ☐ Millet flakes*
- ☐ Rice flakes*
- ☐ Quinoa flakes*
- ☐ Buckwheat flakes*

*Choose these grains only if you require a gluten-free diet.

The Seven-Day Diet recipes are all simple assemblies of ingredients that require minimal preparation and cooking time.

Spices, flavorings, and oils

- ☐ Cold-pressed olive oil
- ☐ Cold-pressed sesame oil

- ☐ Yeast-free vegetable bouillon
- ☐ Mango powder, available from spice shops or Indian food shops (or substitute fresh lemon juice)

- ☐ Ground nutmeg
- ☐ Ground cinnamon
- ☐ Cardamom (ground or pods)
- ☐ Caraway seeds
- ☐ Cumin seeds
- ☐ Coriander seeds
- ☐ Garam masala or curry powder
- ☐ Black peppercorns
- ☐ Cayenne pepper
- ☐ Paprika
- ☐ Tahini paste
- ☐ Tumeric

Canned foods

- ☐ 1 can mixed beans†
- ☐ 1 can lentils†
- ☐ 2 cans chickpeas†
- ☐ 2 cans plum tomatoes†
- ☐ 2 cans tuna in spring water, unless you prefer to cook fresh

†I have chosen canned food for simplicity; you can use dried legumes or fresh tomatoes but allow for extra soaking and cooking time if you do.

Fresh vegetables

- ☐ 4 medium onions
- ☐ 1 small red onion
- ☐ 1 pumpkin or winter squash
- ☐ 10 carrots
- ☐ 8 oz (225g) spinach
- ☐ Small bulb fennel
- ☐ 2 small or 1 large head celery
- ☐ 2 medium leeks
- ☐ 2 heads bok choy
- ☐ 4 small heads broccoli
- ☐ 1 small green cabbage

- ☐ 2in (5cm) fresh ginger
- ☐ 6 lemons
- ☐ 2 bulbs garlic

Salad vegetables

- ☐ 12 small/cherry tomatoes
- ☐ 4 medium tomatoes, if not using canned
- ☐ 1 bag of mixed green salad
- ☐ 1 avocado
- ☐ 1 cucumber
- ☐ 3 peppers, yellow, red, or orange
- ☐ 1 bunch of watercress

Frozen foods

- ☐ 2oz (50g) frozen peas
- ☐ 4 large frozen shrimp, if not using fresh

Refrigerated foods

- ☐ 1 lb (450g) low-fat cottage cheese
- ☐ 6 oz (175g) tofu
- ☐ 8 oz (225g) plain yogurt (with active cultures)
- ☐ 8 oz (225g) hummus, or make your own fresh (see recipe, p.26)
- ☐ 1 small carton of milk

- ☐ 4 large shrimp, if not using frozen
- ☐ 4 oz (100g) white fish

- ☐ 6 free-range eggs

Fresh herbs

- ☐ Basil
- ☐ Mint
- ☐ Parsley
- ☐ Cilantro
- ☐ Dill
- ☐ Rosemary
- ☐ Bay leaves
- ☐ Thyme

Food to buy during the week

- ☐ 6 medium tomatoes for day six, if not using canned tomatoes
- ☐ 10oz (300g) salmon fillet for dinner on day five and lunch on day six

Changes that may take place

The Seven-Day Diet is designed to encourage better overall digestion by excluding the three S's—simple carbohydrates, stimulants, and saturated fats. Since your usual diet may include some or all of these elements, it is important to stay aware of what is happening to your body during the seven days, and what these changes mean.

CHILDREN AND PREGNANT WOMEN

I do not recommend that children follow any diet unless it's absolutely necessary, and then only under the supervision of an appropriate health-care professional. The Seven-Day Diet has been designed for adults, so no one under the age of 18 should undertake this diet plan. Pregnant women should not go on the Seven-Day Diet either, but may follow the Plan for Life *(see p.41)* under a doctor's care.

The state of your health

Some people feel energized while they are on the Seven-Day Diet, finding that they sleep well and have a clear mind. However, even if you don't feel especially good, rest assured that this program is an important first step in achieving your goal of feeling good and eating healthfully. I believe that the more of the three S's you normally eat, the more likely you are to experience any one of the following symptoms:

- Fatigue
- Food cravings
- Bad breath
- Mild diarrhea
- Increased need for sleep
- Breakouts

Not everyone experiences unpleasant symptoms, so don't be put off by these warnings. They are all positive signs that things are changing for the better.

The Seven-Day Diet is a short and simple program that will help cleanse your body of the detrimental effects of the three S's.

Signs of change

These are some of the common symptoms that you may experience during the initial stages of the Seven-Day Diet, depending on how much you have previously indulged in the three S's.

Do you feel more tired than usual?

If you have previously relied on caffeine and simple carbohydrates to give you short-term energy, then removing these substances from your diet will help normalize the way your adrenal glands behave. Instead of triggering adrenaline repeatedly through the day, the adrenal glands should start to respond less often, which will keep the levels of glucose in your blood more even and help you to avoid highs and lows. As this process takes place, you may feel more tired than usual. Don't worry—this feeling will soon pass.

Do you have you need for more sleep?

One key requirement of the Seven-Day Diet is rest, and you may notice that you have an increased need for sleep. For this reason I suggest that you don't make any plans for the week; stay home whenever possible and plan some early nights. A benefit: Many people find that they sleep really deeply during the Seven-Day Diet.

Are you craving sugary foods?

You will probably find that if you have eaten simple carbohydrates for energy in the past you are now craving sugar and sweet foods. Such foods have encouraged the unfriendly bacteria and yeasts in your gut to proliferate *(see pp.8–11)*, and since you are removing the simple sugars they feed on by following this diet—in effect starving them—they can become a little demanding! If you do experience any food cravings, they should pass quickly.

Does your breath smell?

Rather than being hindered by the three S's and processed foods, your digestive system is being encouraged to function more efficiently. As a result you may find that you develop a green or white coating on your tongue *(see p.8)*. This may be accompanied by bad breath. Don't worry; this is only temporary. Chewing parsley can help alleviate bad breath, as can cleaning your teeth and gargling with a sugar-free mouthwash.

Are you experiencing mild diarrhea?

The increase in liquids (including water and soups) and fiber that this diet provides can stimulate bowel movements and soften stools. This is a healthy sign that the Seven-Day Diet is having an effect. Conversely, some people get slightly constipated for the first day or two, but this, too, is likely to be temporary.

Have you broken out?

It is possible that you may develop some pimples or other blemishes, especially around the chin. This suggests that your digestive system is undergoing a mild cleansing, and is a great sign that things are changing. Bear with the problem; it won't last long.

Seven-day diet
soups

These soups are an integral part of the Seven-Day Diet for several reasons. The clear soup is a highly concentrated, cleansing drink rich in minerals, designed to help improve the workings of the digestive system as quickly as possible. This soup will be used throughout the week to increase your fluid intake.

The vegetable-based soups provide your body with a high degree of easily absorbed nutrients, together with vital fiber and liquid. They will also help to promote better digestive health, which is the main goal of the Food Doctor eating plan.

The soups are all easy to prepare by even the most inexperienced cook and can be stored in the refrigerator for up to a week, or in the freezer. Try to make these soups one day ahead of beginning the Seven-Day Diet. If you work, use a thermos to take your soups along for healthy breaks during the day.

Clear soup
for the 14 snacks in the Seven-Day Diet

4 carrots, roughly chopped
½ small head celery, roughly chopped
1 medium onion, quartered
2 cloves garlic
14 cups water
3 sprigs fresh parsley, chopped
Large handful fresh spinach, shredded
Pinch cayenne pepper (or more if desired)
Fresh lemon juice to taste

Put the carrots, celery, onion, and garlic in a large saucepan. Add the water, bring the soup to a boil, cover, and simmer over low heat for 20 minutes.

Add the parsley and shredded spinach and simmer for 10 minutes more. Turn off the heat and strain the soup through a sieve into a large bowl, then discard the vegetables. Flavor the soup with cayenne pepper and a few squeezes of lemon juice if you want the soup to have a bit of a kick. Store in the refrigerator for the duration of the diet.

Tomato and rosemary soup

for three meals on days one, two, and three

1 medium onion, diced
2 ribs celery, sliced
1 carrot, diced
1 large clove garlic, crushed
1 14oz (400g) can plum tomatoes, chopped
1 sprig fresh rosemary
1 flat teaspoon mango powder, or the juice of ½ lemon
4 cups fresh chicken or vegetable stock, or add 1 tablespoon yeast-free bouillon powder to 4 cups water
Large handful shredded spinach
1 medium head bok choy, shredded

Heat two tablespoons of olive oil in a large saucepan. Add the onion, celery, carrot, and garlic and cook gently over low heat until the vegetables begin to soften. Stir in the tomatoes and add the rosemary and mango powder or lemon juice. Simmer for five minutes, then add the stock, cover, and simmer for 15 minutes or so, until the vegetables are cooked but not mushy.

Stir in the spinach and bok choy and cook for two or three minutes more until they wilt. Remove the rosemary and season with freshly ground black pepper. Divide the soup into three individual portions and store in the refrigerator.

Chunky vegetable soup

for three meals on days four, six, and seven

1 teaspoon each of caraway and cumin seeds
1 medium onion, diced
1 clove garlic, crushed
½ lb (225g) pumpkin or winter squash such as acorn or butternut, peeled and cut into small cubes
½ small green cabbage, shredded
1 small head broccoli, broken into florets
1 stick celery, sliced
1 small carrot, diced
½ medium leek, finely sliced
6 cups fresh chicken or vegetable stock, or add 1½ tablespoons yeast-free bouillon powder to 6 cups water
1 bay leaf

Put the seeds in a small, heavy pan and toast over medium heat for a few minutes until lightly browned.

Gently heat two tablespoons of olive oil in a large pan and soften the onion and garlic for five minutes. Add the rest of the vegetables and the seeds. Heat them together in the oil for another five minutes or so, then add just enough stock to cover the vegetables and simmer for ten minutes. Add the remaining stock and the bay leaf, season with black pepper and simmer, covered, for about 20 minutes until all the vegetables are cooked. Divide the soup into three portions and store in the refrigerator or freezer.

Day 1

Breakfast

This meal provides the right mix of ingredients to give your body energy and enable you to have the best start to the day.

Glass of hot water with juice of ½ lemon

Cinnamon oatmeal

RECIPES

2 tablespoons old-fashioned oats
6 tablespoons water
2 tablespoons plain yogurt
Pinch of ground cinnamon

Combine the oats and water in a small saucepan, bring to a boil and simmer for one minute or until the oats are soft.

Turn off the heat and let the oatmeal stand for another minute before serving. Top with the yogurt and a sprinkle of cinnamon.

Midmorning snack

Your breakfast should have lasted you well into the morning but by 10:30AM or so you will probably be feeling hungry enough to need this snack.

1 cup clear soup

2 strips each of red and orange pepper, 1 stalk of celery, and 1 tablespoon of pumpkin seeds

MANAGING YOUR TIME

This diet is based upon fresh, homemade meals, so you need to allow time before each meal to prepare the ingredients and cook your food.

In practice, this really means getting up ten minutes earlier or so each morning. In the evening, you may find that you enjoy the chance to slow your pace and unwind as you prepare dinner.

On day one, you are probably feeling full of good intentions. In fact, this first day shouldn't prove too difficult as your food choices are tasty and varied and you won't begin to feel the effects of your change in eating habits until tonight or tomorrow morning.

Remember to drink plenty of water and herbal teas in between meals, and try to rest in the evening. All menus in the Seven-Day Diet Plan serve one.

Lunch

Assuming that you ate your mid-morning snack about 10:30AM, you should eat lunch around 1:00PM, so that your energy levels stay constant.

Broccoli and tomato salad with tofu or tuna

Midafternoon snack

Eating in the afternoon is really important since the gap between lunch and dinner can be a long one. Eat this snack around 4:00PM.

1 cup clear soup

Plain cottage cheese on 1 rye crispbread, topped with a pinch of garam masala or curry powder

Dinner

This meal is quick and convenient if you made your soups in advance, or cook a batch of soup now *(see p.23)* and store the rest in the refrigerator.

Tomato and rosemary soup with mixed beans or sliced omelet

Juice of ½ lemon
Pinch ground black pepper
1 oz (25g) tofu or 2 oz (50g) canned tuna
Handful broccoli florets
4 small tomatoes, halved

Mix a marinade of lemon juice in a small bowl and season with freshly ground black pepper.

If you are using tofu, cut it into cubes and add to the marinade.

If you are using tuna, separate the flakes loosely with a fork and add to the marinade.

Place the broccoli and tomatoes in a bowl, scatter the tofu or tuna over the top, drizzle with olive oil, and serve.

Store extra tofu or tuna in the refrigerator for lunch on day four.

MEALS TO GO

If you work in an office or are away from home most days, you may be wondering how you will manage to stick to the diet. Why not prepare your snacks and lunch the night before or first thing in the morning and pack it into plastic containers? You can also heat your soup in the morning and bring it into work in a thermos.

Be sure to take a break from work to eat so that the stress of the day doesn't impair your digestion.

1½ cups tomato and rosemary soup
2 tablespoons mixed beans, canned or soaked and cooked, or 1 egg
Pinch of turmeric

If you are using mixed beans, ladle the soup into a saucepan and add the beans. Warm over low heat and serve.

If you are using an egg, beat it with a tablespoon of water and season with freshly ground pepper and turmeric.

Lightly oil an omelet pan using a little olive oil on a paper towel. Pour in the egg mixture and cook over low heat until it sets. Flip the egg over and cook on the other side until golden. Place the omelet on a wooden board or plate; when cool, roll up and cut into thin rounds. Heat the soup through, stir in the sliced omelet and serve.

Day 2

Don't give in to temptation. The cleansing effects of this diet are now under way, improving your digestion. Once again, be sure that you have plenty of water to drink, perhaps flavored with some sliced cucumber or a squeeze of fresh lime.

If this is a work day, remember to prepare your snacks and lunch to take in with you so that you can stick to the plan.

Breakfast

Ideally you should eat within an hour of waking to replenish energy stores that have been depleted overnight. Today's breakfast is quick and easy.

**Glass of hot water
with juice of ½ lemon**

Three-seed yogurt

RECIPES

3 tablespoons plain yogurt
1 tablespoon pumpkin seeds
1 tablespoon sunflower seeds
1 heaped teaspoon sesame seeds
Pinch of ground cinnamon

Spoon three generous tablespoons of yogurt into a bowl. Sprinkle the pumpkin, sunflower, and sesame seeds over the top. Flavor with a pinch of cinnamon and serve.

Midmorning snack

A midmorning snack helps you to make it through to lunchtime. This combination will sustain you until your next meal.

1 cup clear soup

Hummus spread on 1 rice cake

15oz (425g) chickpeas
2 tablespoons tahini paste
2 tablespoons lemon juice
1 clove garlic, crushed
Olive oil and cayenne pepper to garnish

Blend the chick-peas, tahini, lemon juice, garlic, and some freshly ground black pepper to a smooth paste in a food processor. Scrape into a small bowl, drizzle with a little olive oil, and sprinkle with cayenne pepper. Cover and keep refrigerated.

Spread a rice cake with one tablespoon of the hummus for your snack.

Save two tablespoons of chickpeas for dinner tonight if you want to add them to your soup.

Lunch

If you made your frittata first thing this morning before going out for the day, eat it cold or reheat it if you can. Take time chewing each mouthful.

Vegetable frittata

Midafternoon snack

Like your midmorning snack, this combination of nuts and raw vegetables should help you to feel satisfied until dinner.

1 cup clear soup

10 cashew nuts, 2 thick slices of cucumber, 2 strips of pepper

Dinner

All evening meals consist of protein and vegetables. You don't need to eat carbohydrates this late in the day as you will not use the energy they give.

Tomato and rosemary soup with chickpeas or flaked fish

1 small red onion, finely chopped
1 clove garlic, crushed
2 eggs
1 tablespoon live plain yogurt
½ teaspoon paprika
1 tablespoon chopped parsley
½ teaspoon chopped thyme
2 tablespoons frozen peas
1 medium ripe tomato, chopped

Gently soften the onion and garlic in a tablespoon of olive oil in a small frying pan over a low heat. Beat the eggs with the yogurt and paprika, add the herbs, season with black pepper, and pour into the pan. Scatter the peas and tomato on top, cook gently until the eggs set, then turn out onto a plate and serve.

Set a small serving of frittata aside for your midafternoon snack tomorrow.

WHAT CAN I DRINK?

This diet, though very short, depends on some basic rules that will make the difference between feeling great at the end or not noticing much change at all. One important rule is to avoid alcohol, tea, and coffee. This may sound impossible, but try it and see—you will probably find that you sleep better, wake up feeling refreshed, and experience fewer energy slumps. Drink at least eight large glasses of water through the day to stay hydrated.

2 tablespoons chickpeas or
4oz (100g) white fish fillet, cut into bite-sized pieces
Juice of ½ lemon
1 teaspoon ground coriander
1½ cups tomato and rosemary soup

If you are using chickpeas, add two tablespoons of cooked chickpeas to the soup before heating it thoroughly in a saucepan over a low heat.

If you are using fish, let it marinate in the lemon juice, coriander, and freshly ground black pepper while you ladle the soup into a saucepan and heat it thoroughly. Add the fish and simmer for five minutes or until just cooked, and then serve.

Day 3

You are now nearing the halfway point of the diet, so you should be feeling a little lighter—and hopefully less hungry, too. Don't feel tempted to stray from the recommended foods, and avoid overeating at mealtimes.

If you are going to be out and about today, take one portion of tomato and rosemary soup out of the refrigerator first thing in the morning and blend it until smooth in a processor.

Breakfast

Eggs are a great source of protein for breakfast. Boil your egg according to personal preference; the ideal time to cook a soft-boiled egg is four minutes.

Glass of hot water with juice of ½ lemon

1 boiled egg with 2 rice cakes

RECIPES

EXCLUSION ZONE

You may have noticed that the Seven-Day Diet excludes meat. This is because I believe that the saturated fats in meat—and especially in red meat—promote the proliferation of unfriendly bacteria and potential yeast in the gut *(see pp.8–11, p.50)*. Since these fats are detrimental to your overall digestive health in large quantities, meat is not an option on the Seven-Day Diet.

Midmorning snack

If you work in an office, make the cucumber-mint yogurt in advance so that you can take it in to work with you and store it in the refrigerator.

1 cup clear soup

Cucumber-mint yogurt on 2 melba toasts

¼ cucumber, peeled and grated
2 tablespoons plain yogurt
Sprig or two of fresh mint, shredded

Mix the cucumber and yogurt. Add the mint, season with freshly ground black pepper, and mix well.

Spread on two melba toasts and serve with the soup.

Lunch

This is the last portion of the tomato and rosemary soup, so blending it to a smooth texture will make it taste slightly different.

Smooth tomato and rosemary soup with yogurt

Midafternoon snack

For this instant afternoon snack, take the slice of frittata left over from yesterday's lunch out of the refrigerator and eat it cold.

1 cup clear soup

1 small slice of frittata with 2 small tomatoes

Dinner

This meal is very nutritious and will take you about 25 minutes to cook. Remember to save a spoonful of pesto for tomorrow morning's snack.

Quinoa with pesto and roast tomatoes

1½ cups tomato and rosemary soup
1 tablespoon plain yogurt

Blend the soup in a food processor and then heat it thoroughly in a small pan over low heat.

Pour the hot soup into a bowl and swirl the yogurt into it just before serving.

FRUIT-FREE WEEK

Fruit is also off-limits on the Seven-Day Diet for the simple reason that it contains a form of sugar. The natural sugar in fruit, known as fructose, can act like all other sugars in some ways as it may encourage the growth of unfriendly bacteria and yeast in the gut. The aim of this diet is to make your digestive system as healthy as possible, so fruit is off the menu for the duration of these seven days only.

2 medium tomatoes
2 sprigs fresh rosemary
For the pesto:
  1 large handful fresh basil
  ½ cup olive oil
  4oz (100g) pine nuts
  1 small clove garlic
2oz (50g) quinoa
½ cup water with ½ teaspoon of yeast-free bouillon powder added

Preheat the oven to 400°F/200°C. Put the tomatoes and rosemary in a baking dish, drizzle with olive oil, and roast for 20 minutes. Meanwhile, blend the pesto ingredients in a food processor. Simmer the quinoa and water in a pan until soft, stir in three teaspoons of pesto and serve with the tomatoes (remove the rosemary sprigs first). Store the remaining pesto in the refrigerator.

Day 4

Today you will continue to eat lightly, so try to stay busy doing something you enjoy.

If you have already cooked and frozen the chunky vegetable soup, take a portion out of the freezer first thing in the morning and let it defrost in the refrigerator during the day ready for dinner. Rest in the evening and go to bed early if you feel tired.

Breakfast

Oatmeal aids the efficient functioning of your digestive system and provides much-needed energy to get you through the morning.

Glass of hot water with juice of ½ lemon

Nutmeg oatmeal

RECIPES

2 tablespoons old-fashioned oats
¼ cup water
2 tablespoons plain yogurt
Pinch of ground nutmeg

Combine the oats and water in a small saucepan, bring to a boil, then simmer for one minute until softened.

Let the oatmeal stand off the heat for another minute, then serve. Top with the yogurt and nutmeg.

Midmorning snack

Use the pesto you saved from last night's meal for this snack. Squeeze a little lemon juice over the top to lift the flavors.

1 cup clear soup

Pesto spread on 1 rice cake

Spread a rice cake with a generous helping of pesto and enjoy with your hot soup.

Lunch

Take time to sit down and eat your lunch slowly without any stress. Chewing properly will also help you digest your food.

Pepper and bok choy salad with tuna or tofu

Midafternoon snack

This energizing snack will help you avoid the midafternoon slump in energy that often follows lunch or a busy morning's work.

1 cup clear soup

10 cashew nuts, 5 small florets of broccoli, and 2 small tomatoes

Dinner

Eat dinner early in the evening. You should allow for a minimum of at least two hours in between eating and going to bed.

Chunky vegetable soup with mixed beans or sliced omelet

Pinch of garam masala or curry powder
½ red or yellow pepper, cut in strips
1oz (25g) tofu, cut into bite-sized pieces, or 2oz (50g) canned tuna from day one
Juice of ½ lemon
1 small head bok choy, shredded
1 tablespoon grated carrot
½ teaspoon poppy seeds

Combine the lemon juice and garam masala or curry powder in a small bowl and season with freshly ground black pepper. Add the tofu or tuna to this marinade and marinate for a few minutes.

Put the pepper and bok choy in a salad bowl and toss in a dressing of olive oil and freshly ground black pepper. Top with the carrot and poppy seeds. Arrange the tuna or tofu with marinade on the salad, and serve.

SHOP FOR THE NEXT FEW MEALS

Look ahead now to tomorrow's menu to make sure that you have all the ingredients you will need.

You will need to buy some fresh salmon today or tomorrow in time for your evening meal. You may also need to buy a few extra vegetables and more plain yogurt if you have run out.

1½ cups chunky vegetable soup
2 tablespoons mixed beans, canned or soaked and cooked, or 1 egg
Pinch of turmeric

If you are using mixed beans, ladle the soup into a saucepan and add the beans. Warm through over low heat and serve.

If you are using an egg, beat it with a tablespoon of water and season with freshly ground pepper and turmeric.

Lightly oil an omelet pan using a little olive oil on a paper towel. Pour in the egg mixture and cook over a low heat until it sets. Flip the egg and cook on the other side until golden. Place the omelet on a wooden board or plate; when cool, roll up and cut into thin rounds. Heat the soup through, stir in the sliced omelet and serve.

Day 5

You are now past the halfway point and your body is responding to the diet. You may also notice some of the physical changes described on pages 20–21.

There are only three more days to go, so resist temptation. If it is the weekend, keep yourself busy with an activity you enjoy and concentrate on your sense of well-being.

Breakfast

Flaxseeds are a valuable addition to your diet; they encourage regular bowel movements and provide essential nutrients.

**Glass of hot water
with juice of ½ lemon**

**Soaked flaxseeds
with plain yogurt**

RECIPES

1 tablespoon flaxseeds
3 tablespoons plain yogurt
Pinch of ground cinnamon

Soak the flaxseeds overnight in just enough water to cover.

In the morning, drain the water away and combine the seeds with the yogurt. Serve with a sprinkle of cinnamon on top.

Midmorning snack

If you need to make this snack in advance, squeeze lemon juice over the avocado to prevent it from turning brown, and refrigerate.

1 cup clear soup

**Avocado spread on 1 rye
crispbread with chopped tomato**

½ small avocado
Juice of ¼ lemon
Freshly ground black pepper, to taste
1 small tomato, chopped

Combine the avocado, lemon juice, and black pepper in a bowl and mash together with a fork.

Spread the mixture on one rye crispbread, scatter the chopped tomato over the top, and serve with the soup.

Lunch

This recipe is designed to be tasty and satisfying, so beware of increasing the portion size according to how hungry you think you might be.

Quick chickpea stew

Midafternoon snack

Eating this snack at about the same time each day keeps your energy levels constant so that you don't feel tempted to stray from the diet.

1 cup clear soup

Tuna dip with celery, carrot sticks, or fennel.

Dinner

Don't forget to save a spoonful of spinach and a small portion of salmon for tomorrow. Alternatively, you may prefer a poached egg with the spinach.

Spinach with herb salmon or poached egg

1 tablespoon olive oil

½ teaspoon cumin seeds

1 teaspoon cardamom seeds, ground *(see p.129),* or cardamom powder

1 medium onion, chopped

2 cloves garlic, crushed

14oz (400g) ripe or canned tomatoes, chopped

15oz (425g) canned chickpeas

2 cups water

Heat the olive oil in a medium saucepan on low heat, add the spices, and cook one minute. Add the onion and garlic, soften for five minutes, then stir in the tomatoes and chickpeas. Pour in the water and simmer 10–15 minutes, stirring occasionally, until the sauce thickens. Serve two tablespoons of stew with a salad dressed with olive oil and lemon juice. Refrigerate the remaining stew.

1 oz (25g) canned tuna

2 tablespoons plain yogurt

Sprigs of fresh parsley, chopped

Pinch of cayenne pepper

Mash the tuna with the yogurt, season with freshly ground black pepper, and stir in the chopped parsley.

Scoop up the dip with celery, carrot sticks, or fennel, and sprinkle a little cayenne pepper on top before serving with the soup.

10oz (275g) salmon fillet or 1 egg

Handful of chopped dill, cilantro, or parsley

Juice of ¼ lemon

Freshly ground black pepper

1 clove of garlic, finely chopped

4oz (100g) fresh spinach, washed

Pinch of garam masala or curry powder

If you are using salmon, preheat the oven to 350°F/180°C. Coat the fish in the herbs, place on an oiled sheet of foil, and season with lemon juice, black pepper, and garlic. Fold the ends of the foil to seal. Bake for 20 minutes. If you are using an egg, poach it in boiling water until set.

Put the spinach in a medium saucepan and cook over gentle heat until wilted. Drain well. Drizzle with sesame oil, lemon juice, and garam masala or curry powder. Top with the salmon or egg and serve.

Day 6

You are almost there, so persevere for these last two days and you will soon be reaping the benefits.

If you have frozen your home-made soup, then take the last two portions out of the freezer first thing this morning and let them defrost in the refrigerator over the course of the day.

Take things easy if you are tired—although some people feel energized by this stage.

Breakfast

If you are following a gluten-free diet, make sure you choose those grains marked with an asterisk* when you mix up your muesli.

Glass of hot water with juice of ½ lemon

Muesli with whole milk or plain yogurt

RECIPES

Choose 1 tablespoon each from any four of the following grains:
  Barley flakes
  Rye flakes
  Oat flakes
  Millet flakes*
  Rice flakes*
  Quinoa flakes*
  Buckwheat flakes*
8–9 mixed nuts: hazelnuts, cashew nuts, brazil nuts, almonds, walnuts
1 teaspoon raisins
½ cup whole milk

Combine the dry ingredients in a bowl, add your choice of milk (either whole cow's, goat's or sheep's milk or an unsweetened substitute such as rice or soy milk) or one tablespoon of live plain yogurt and serve.

Midmorning snack

Use the extra spoonful of spinach from last night's meal for this snack. Squeeze over a little lemon juice if you want to lift the flavours slightly.

1 cup clear soup

Spinach and yogurt on 1 melba toast, seasoned with a pinch of cayenne pepper

Chop the spinach and spread it on one oatcake. Top with a teaspoon of yogurt and sprinkle with a little cayenne pepper before serving with the soup.

Lunch

If you had salmon for dinner last night, then use the remaining fish in this salad. If you had a poached egg, slice up an avocado instead.

Avocado or cold salmon with watercress salad

Midafternoon snack

Any cravings you may have had for sweet, sugary food should have passed by now, so enjoy this sustaining snack.

1 cup clear soup

Cottage cheese spread on 1 rice cake, topped with chopped fresh cilantro

Dinner

Add a spoonful of yesterday's quick chickpea stew to tonight's soup, or include a few cooked shrimp instead if you prefer.

Chunky vegetable soup with chickpeas or prawns

½ teaspoon cumin seeds
Handful of fresh watercress, arugula, Bibb lettuce, or other salad greens
1 teaspoon olive oil
Juice of ¼ lemon
Freshly ground black pepper to taste
4 small tomatoes, halved
½ avocado, sliced, or cold salmon

Toast the cumin seeds gently in a small heavy-bottomed saucepan for one minute, then remove from the heat.

Dress the salad with a drizzle of olive oil, lemon juice, freshly ground black pepper, and the dry-roasted cumin seeds. Add the tomatoes, mix well, and serve with the salmon or avocado.

EXERCISE

It is fine to exercise while you are on the Seven-Day Diet, but don't overexert yourself, and allow time to rest afterward. Time your exercise to fit in before a snack or meal so that you can refuel quickly and not feel hungry.

Don't attempt any unfamiliar sports or workouts while you are on this diet. The unfamiliar exercise may exhaust you or prove to be excessive.

1¼ cups chunky vegetable soup
4 large cooked shrimp
or 1 tablespoon quick chickpea stew

Pour the soup into a saucepan and add the shrimp or chickpea stew. Heat thoroughly over low heat and serve.

Day 7

Congratulations—it's your last day! I hope that you found the diet easy to follow and that by now you are feeling well, energized, and inspired to move on to the next stage, Plan for Life *(see pp.38–91)*.

Breakfast

Continue the routine of preparing a nutritious, well-balanced breakfast of protein and carbohydrates such as this after you finish the diet.

Glass of hot water with juice of ½ lemon

Scrambled egg with 1 melba toast

RECIPES

1 egg
1 teaspoon plain yogurt
Freshly ground black pepper to taste
Pinch of turmeric
Drizzle of olive oil
Sprig of fresh parsley, chopped
1 melba toast

Beat together the egg and the yogurt, then season with freshly ground black pepper and add a pinch of ground turmeric powder.

Heat a little olive oil in a small saucepan, pour in the beaten egg, and cook over low heat until the egg forms soft curds. Once cooked, stir in the parsley and serve with the melba toast.

Midmorning snack

If you made your own hummus on day two, use up the rest of it for this crunchy snack. Otherwise use store-bought hummus.

1 cup clear soup

1 tablespoon of hummus with raw vegetables

1 tablespoon hummus
Small selection of raw vegetables such as carrots, fennel, or celery, sliced

Serve with the soup, using the vegetables to scoop up the hummus.

Lunch

Add a few pieces of tofu or some pumpkin seeds to this final serving of your homemade soup in order to vary the flavor.

Chunky vegetable soup with tofu or pumpkin seeds

Midafternoon snack

This is the last of the nutrient-rich clear soup that has helped cleanse and improve your digestive system to give you a fresh start.

1 cup clear soup

Cottage cheese spread on 1 rye crispbread

Dinner

Use up your remaining vegetables for this stir-fry and add pumpkin seeds or the leftover tofu you saved from lunchtime.

Stir-fried vegetables with marinated tofu or pumpkin seeds

1½ cups chunky vegetable soup
2oz (50g) tofu, finely cubed,
or 1 heaped teaspoon pumpkin seeds

Pour the soup into a saucepan and warm it gently over low heat. Add the tofu or pumpkin seeds, transfer to a bowl, and serve.

Store the rest of the tofu in the fridge for tonight's supper.

THE BENEFITS OF THE SEVEN-DAY DIET

As you come to the end of the Seven-Day Diet, you should hopefully feel some or all of the following:

- Improved digestion
- Sense of well-being
- More energy
- Reduced sugar cravings
- Reduced cravings for caffeine and alcohol
- Enhanced absorption of nutrients

About 6 oz (175g) various vegetables such as carrots, peppers, leeks, and broccoli
2 tablespoons lemon juice
½ teaspoon fresh ginger, grated
1 teaspoon cardamom seeds, ground *(see p.129)*, or cardamom powder
Freshly ground black pepper to taste
2oz (50g) tofu, finely cubed,
or 1 heaped teaspoon pumpkin seeds
Drizzle of sesame oil

Slice the vegetables finely. Mix the lemon juice, ginger, cardamom, and pepper in a bowl. Add the vegetables and tofu (if using) and let stand for 15 minutes.

Heat a tablespoon of water in a wok, add the vegetables, and stir-fry quickly over high heat until just cooked but crisp. Drizzle with sesame oil. If using pumpkin seeds, sprinkle them in just before serving.

Plan for life

The Plan for Life is a simple, sustainable eating program that is designed to be adapted to your individual lifestyle. It is important that you read through this whole section before starting so that you understand and become familiar with the ten basic Food Doctor principles—the essential guidelines on how to eat for health and well-being. Once you begin to incorporate the principles into your own schedule you may want to plan ahead to make sure you have the appropriate foods for the right meals, but this plan should soon become second nature to you.

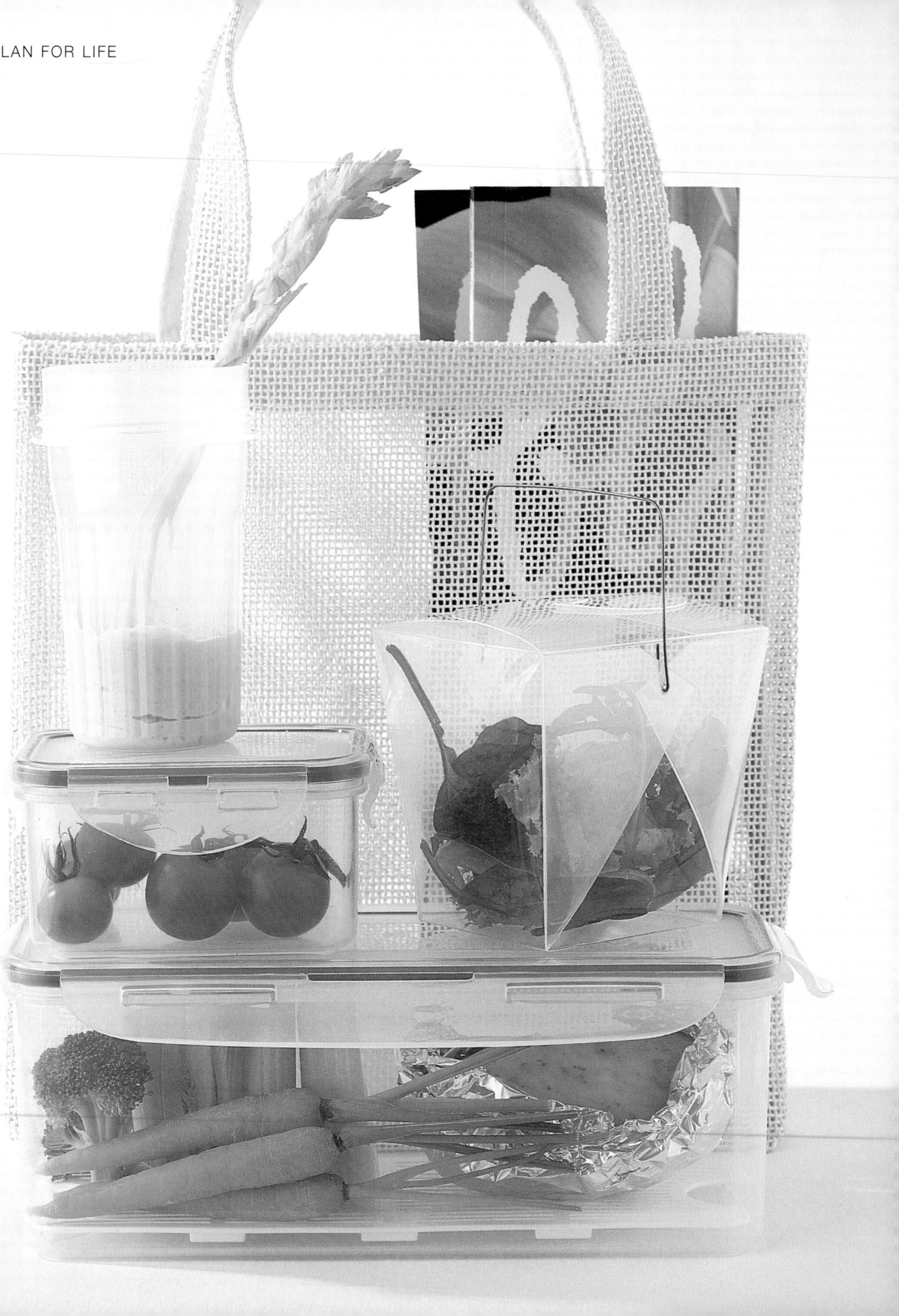

Eating for life

Any diet plan should be a sensible one that incorporates all the best that food can offer, from nutrients and fiber to flavor. I believe that the steady process of safe, sustainable weight loss and healthy eating advocated by the Plan for Life will help you feel and look your best.

The Plan for Life program shows you how to eat well with plenty of choice, how to lose weight and yet still be able to enjoy special occasions and have a social life. It even allows you to veer away from time to time to enjoy your favorite treat.

The following pages reveal ten crucial Food Doctor principles and explain how and why changes in your diet may need to be made, and what you can expect as a result of those changes. The principles cover several areas, including how to combine foods effectively, what to drink, when to eat for maximum energy, and how to avoid hunger. I am confident that this set of principles will provide a solid base for you to apply to your own lifestyle so that you develop good eating habits.

Plan of action

It may be that some of the principles are familiar to you, or that a few of them are already a part of your daily life, but it is important that you incorporate these principles as a group if you want to reap the greatest benefits. I suggest that you read through this section first before introducing each principle, one at a time, over a period of weeks. Thus, during week one you can make changes in line with Principle 1, then after a few days introduce Principle 2, and so on. Within a month you will find that you have made some real changes, but don't rush it or you will set yourself up to fail. I have seen too many diets falter and good intentions fly out of the window because people set unrealistic goals that made the whole process daunting.

If you feel that you have a lot of weight to lose, then aim to lose a few pounds each month, which is, after all, how you gained the weight in the first place. Similarly, if you want to shed only a few pounds then that, too,

should be undertaken slowly. You probably know from experience that fast weight-loss is unsustainable; if you do manage to lose weight then you inevitably gain it—and more—back again before too long.

The amount of weight you want to lose is, in many ways, up to you. By sticking to the plan 100 percent of the time while maintaining an appropriate level of exercise, you will achieve maximum weight loss. However, if this approach proves hard to sustain, why not think of this plan as a life-changing experience that will improve your health and self-image while still giving you a chance to eat what you like once in a while *(see pp.68–69)*?

The Plan for Life should suit almost every lifestyle. It has been designed to reduce your levels of hunger, it's easy to follow and you don't have to buy obscure foods. Remember, too, that packaged and convenience foods are often far higher in sugar and saturated fats than any meals you make at home. However convenient they may be, they are for emergencies only, not for every day.

WHAT IF I'M PREGNANT?

I do not recommend dieting if you are pregnant as weight gain associated with pregnancy is a natural and important process. However, the Food Doctor plan is a plan for life so you can follow it under the supervision of your doctor, even if you are pregnant or nursing. Do not watch your weight, just eat well. Eat fresh foods, cook for yourself when you can, avoid stimulants and processed foods, and you should find that you do not gain excess weight, only what is natural during pregnancy. There will be plenty of time to lose weight after your baby is born.

Shopping for the plan for life

Unless you are lucky enough to live near a wonderful market, shopping for food is not always the most enthralling pastime. Yet if you allow for a little extra time when you shop, you may be tempted by a whole range of healthy, delicious foods you never noticed before.

With time now at such a premium, most of us consider food shopping to be a time-consuming, repetitive chore that prevents us from doing something else more interesting. It's all too easy to assume that the process of shopping, cooking, and eating is not worth spending our precious time on.

Ever-increasing sales of ready-made foods tend to reflect this growing attitude, and yet the sort of food I believe we should all be eating doesn't come packaged in boxes with microwave instructions. It's likely that if you have gained weight in the past you will be familiar with these types of processed meals. The truth is that a basic homemade meal takes far less time to prepare than you might think, and it invariably tastes much more delicious than ready-made food *(see box, below)*.

Change your shopping habits

Try this simple test at home. Make a list of all the foods you usually buy, including treats, low-fat alternatives, canned drinks, and ready-made meals, and file it away. Then take a look at the recommended carbohydrates and proteins for the Plan for Life *(see pp.50–53)* and make a new shopping list for yourself using those charts as a template. You will see that most of the foods listed are familiar. Your supermarket probably stocks a majority

of these foods, yet for one reason or another they haven't caught your attention before. As you shop, familiarize yourself with these different products and stock up with them for your new eating plan.

Should I buy organic food?

In the same way that the term "low fat" has come to imply "healthy," labeling food as organic can suggest added benefits. Organic fruit and vegetables are generally more expensive that nonorganic alternatives, and if you can afford them, or choose to make them part of your shopping list, go ahead and buy them. However, the organic nature of fruit and vegetables isn't going to make a significant difference to the success of this plan. Many of us fail to eat the recommended five portions of fruits and vegetables a day, but it is better to eat five nonorganic varieties than two or three organic ones.

When it comes to poultry, meat, and fish, however, I do believe that there is a difference. These foods have been devalued, and we expect not to have to pay that much for them. Organic meat is produced using traditional methods of raising animals, hence the higher cost—and better flavor. While an organic chicken may be twice as expensive as a regular one, the flavour alone is worth the extra money. You are likely to value it far more and enjoy eating it as well.

Ordinary grocery-store meat, unlike organic meat, is not guaranteed to be free of chemical residues, antibiotics, and hormones, so it's no wonder that the flavor might not be exciting. It also means that you probably add breadcrumbs, fatty sauces, or side dishes to make the meal more interesting.

So bear in mind that shopping for better-quality foods encourages a healthier relationship with eating, potentially giving you a clearer palate that will allow you to taste and enjoy all the ingredients in your meals.

MAKE YOUR OWN CONVENIENCE FOOD

Homemade soup is a great example of a convenient, healthy meal that can be frozen and then thawed quickly *(see pp.123–24)*. After all, what could be more instant than warming some soup quickly and adding a can of beans and some fresh herbs? Soup is a delicious, easy meal with a good balance of carbohydrates, fiber, and protein.

Which is best?

Convenience food

I have noticed that many people who battle with their weight eat more convenience foods than fresh, homemade food. The levels of sugars and fats in these meals are a large part of the problem. By all means keep a few prepared foods in the freezer for emergencies, but eat them only occasionally, when you have no other choice.

Canned food

I have no problem with canned food: It's cheap, easy to store, and convenient for meals and snacks. However, be sure to buy products that contain no added sugar or salt. Cans of conventional baked beans, for example, contain far more sugar than you might imagine, so look for varieties that are low in sugar. It's also worth having some cans of vegetables on hand, but again, avoid any products that are high in sodium or have added sugar.

Cooking techniques

If you don't consider yourself to be adept in the kitchen, or if you find preparing and cooking food a laborious and boring chore, then it is time to consider how this issue may have contributed to your weight gain. Cooking can be an easy, even enjoyable, pastime.

The plethora of cooking shows and celebrity chefs on television these days is a good indicator of just how much we love cooking—or at least love watching other people cook. I find that every time I watch one of these shows it almost puts me off cooking, as I feel I can't attain the chefs' high standards. However, cooking needn't be complicated and you need fewer ingredients than you might imagine to make a tasty meal. Try the recipes at the back of this book *(see pp.104–37)* and you will find that they are easy to follow and do not take much time to prepare. And I am sure that once the ten principles of the Plan for Life *(see pp.46–73)* have become second nature to you, you will be happy to apply them to preparing and cooking your own food.

Steaming fish and vegetables

Ideally, all vegetables should be lightly steamed, rather than boiled, so that the fiber of the vegetables remains mostly intact. When you steam vegetables, you do so for just a few minutes—less than you might imagine. The colors and flavors of steamed vegetables are also far more appetizing than those that are boiled or overcooked. So investing in a microwave steamer or a small countertop steamer, or even a steamer basket that you just pop over a pan of water, is a wise move.

The good fats in fish are affected by very high temperatures, so steaming is actually a perfect way to cook most fish. It is fast, too—it often takes no more than ten minutes to achieve a perfectly cooked piece of fish.

Poaching in water

Poaching fish or chicken in a pan of water is really very easy, and it is another excellent way of retaining flavor, color, and texture. You can add herbs or bouillon cubes to the cooking water for added flavor. Be vigilant if you use this method, as poached food can easily overcook.

Grilling and roasting

It is all too easy for the essential fats and fiber in food to be impaired if the temperature of your oven or grill is set too high. If you turn your oven or grill to a medium-to-low heat, you will preserve the nutrients in your food and still enjoy delicious results.

Why can't I fry food?

The worst way to cook food is to fry it. The very high temperatures needed for frying affects the quality of essential fats in food and converts the oil you cook with from a stable "good" fat into an unstable "bad" fat. This increases the levels of free radicals—substances that are believed to be involved in heart disease and cancer. Your fat intake will also be higher than it need be as fried food absorbs much of the fat in which it has been cooked. I strongly recommend that you avoid eating fried food in restaurants because of the unusually high quantities of fats most chefs use to enhance flavor. If you are going to fry food, buy a wok and learn how to stir-fry: move the ingredients quickly around the wok and use just a little sunflower or olive oil to cook with. If you keep your cooking methods as fat-free as possible, your meals will be much healthier.

KEEP IT SIMPLE

Cooking needn't be complicated, so I always suggest to people who are reluctant to cook that they try to keep it simple. The principles of the Plan for Life work just as well with a piece of grilled fish and steamed vegetables or a meal of soup and whole-grain bread as they do with a more complicated meal plan containing several courses.

Why is steaming best?

The valuable nutrients in fresh food aren't affected too much by steaming, and the fiber content of vegetables is left mostly intact. Since fiber is vital for maintaining a healthy digestive system, steaming is my preferred and recommended method of cooking to promote optimum digestive health.

Principle 1
Eat protein with complex carbohydrate

The first of the ten essential Food Doctor principles is based on the fact that some foods are converted into glucose quickly, while other foods take longer to break down. By understanding how to combine the right foods in the correct proportions, you will remain full of energy and still be able to lose weight.

The speed at which foods are broken down into glucose for the body to use as fuel is crucial to the Food Doctor plan. Some foods, known as simple carbohydrates, are low in fiber and quickly converted into glucose once they are digested, while protein and high-fiber, complex carbohydrates take longer to be broken down. If you look at the charts on pages 50–53, you will see how the glycemic index (GI) of many foods reflects this speed. By eating only foods that have a slow conversion rate, you will provide your body with a steady supply of energy and prevent excess glucose being stored as fat.

Rather than having to remember the individual GI value of every food, there is an easier way to follow this principle. If you learn to combine the right proportions of protein and fibrous vegetables for every meal and snack, then this plan should work for you. The best way to begin to understand this concept is to look at the food on your plate and ask yourself, "Where is the protein?"

Complete proteins

Proteins contain amino acids, which are, in effect, the building blocks of the body. There are 22 amino acids in total, of which only nine are classified as essential because they cannot be generated by the body and must come from your diet. The nine basic amino acids, known as complete proteins, contain all the elements the body needs to generate the remaining 13 amino acids. Examples of complete proteins include fish, tofu, and eggs.

THE FOOD DOCTOR EQUATION

ANIMAL OR VEGETABLE
COMPLETE PROTEIN

STARCHY OR VEGETABLE
COMPLEX CARBOHYDRATES

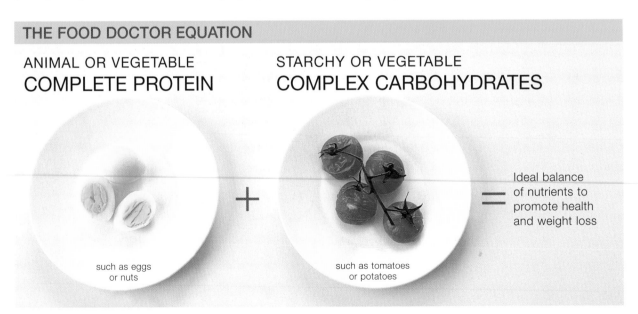

+

=

Ideal balance of nutrients to promote health and weight loss

such as eggs
or nuts

such as tomatoes
or potatoes

The right combination?

protein 0%

complex carbohydrates 90%
of which starch 80%, vegetables 10%

simple carbohydrates 0%

vegetable fat 10%

low in fiber

Whole-wheat pasta with tomato sauce

Although this meal looks healthy, there is no source of protein and the fiber content is low. The proportion of vegetable carbohydrates to starchy carbohydrates (in the form of whole-wheat pasta) is also far too low.

fast

glucose conversion

protein 40%

complex carbohydrates 50%
of which starch 10%, vegetables 40%

simple carbohydrates 0%

vegetable fat 10%

high in fiber

Salmon with broccoli, snowpeas, and whole-wheat pasta

Fish provides the correct amount of protein in this meal, while the proportion of complex vegetable carbohydrates to complex starchy carbohydrates is balanced and the fiber content is substantial.

slow

glucose conversion

Complex versus simple carbohydrates

In the same way that there are two types of protein—complete and incomplete—there are also two types of carbohydrate. A complex carbohydrate is so called because its fiber content remains intact. This means that its natural form has not been interfered with or changed in any way, or, if it has been processed at all, it is by a minimal amount. In contrast, a simple carbohydrate has been processed into a refined product and its fiber is lost. For example, if wheat grain is gently processed into whole-wheat bread, it remains a complex carbohydrate. If the grain is polished more, it becomes a refined product, white bread, which is a simple carbohydrate. The same is true of brown rice or pasta compared to white rice or pasta, or an unsweetened muesli mix compared to a sugared, processed cereal.

When we think of carbohydrates we tend to think of starchy foods such as bread or potatoes, forgetting that fruits and vegetables are also carbohydrates. Complex vegetable carbohydrates are usually dense or green and leafy. However, some fruits can be classed as simple carbohydrates if they have a low fiber content to start with. Since they contain relatively little fiber to slow down the conversion rate from food to glucose, and

The correct proportions?

Lunch proportions

This lunchtime meal shows the ideal ratio of protein to complex carbohydrates. The size of chicken breast you should eat would fit comfortably into the palm of your hand, while vegetables must make up the largest proportion of complex carbohydrates on your plate. This balance of foods should supply just enough nutrients and energy until your mid-afternoon snack.

40% complex carbohydrates
as vegetables

40% protein
as chicken

20% complex carbohydrates
as brown rice

have a naturally high sugar content *(see pp.52–53)*, these fruits are broken down quickly by the body. Examples of soft fruits include watermelons and mangoes. Examples of complex carbohyrdates include most citrus fruits, as well as cruciferous vegetables like broccoli, Brussels sprouts, and cauliflower.

Glycemic Index (GI)

The Glycemic Index (GI) is, in effect, a list of the sugar content of foods. The more quickly a carbohydrate is converted to glucose, the higher the GI score. For example, apple juice is a simple carbohydrate because it is converted rapidly from food to glucose, but a raw apple remains a complex carbohydrate. So the juice has a high score and the raw vegetable has a low score.

Correct ratios

By choosing the correct proportions of complete protein and complex carbohydrates, you can benefit from the energy generated by the slow release of glucose created from each meal or snack, right up until it's time to eat again. Complex carbohydrates also contain plenty of fiber, so each meal or snack helps promote good digestive health as well as energy and weight loss.

Dinner is different

There is just one exception to the rule about meal proportions. If you eat later in the evenings, avoid starchy carbohydrates altogether, since you won't use the energy they create. This means adding extra protein and vegetables to your evening meal so that the ratios are nearer to 50 percent protein and 50 percent vegetables.

I also recommend setting a little portion of food back to snack on later in the evening—even if it's just a mouthful or two. This will make it easier to handle late-night cravings.

50% protein
as fish

50% complex carbohydrates
as vegetables

Protein profiles

The proteins that I recommend you eat on the Plan for Life are all lean proteins, and are also what is known as complete. Remember that complete proteins cannot be generated by the body and must therefore come from your diet. The lean protein foods in the ideal category (*see chart, below*) contain all nine essential proteins.

Can I eat red meat?

I do not consider red meat to be a lean protein, as it contains a higher proportion of saturated fats than, for example, skinless poultry. Saturated fats are not ideal for overall digestive health, as I believe they can promote the proliferation of unfriendly bacteria and yeasts in the intestines. However, red meat is a complete protein and it is a good source of minerals, so eating red meat two or, if absolutely necessary, three times a week is a good way to maintain some variety and interest in your choice of proteins.

Can I eat too much protein?

There is controversy as to whether you can eat too much protein, not least because diet plans based on 100 percent protein plans do lead to weight loss—although the long-term cost to overall health is not yet fully understood. Too much protein can lead to a situation in which minerals are released from the bones to counteract the acidity of the blood. This is a natural occurrence when excess protein is eaten and can lead to reduced bone density. In addition, kidney damage is a risk for some individuals as the kidneys must cope with the added strain of breaking down large amounts of protein. Pure protein diets are by nature low in fresh produce, so fiber and antioxidant intake is low as well.

This is precisely the opposite of the Food Doctor plan, which has been designed to enhance digestive health and includes only about 40 percent protein, thus meeting most people's dietary requirements.

HOW DO I GET THE PROPORTIONS PER SERVING RIGHT?

Rather than weighing food, the best way to work out the correct serving of protein for a meal is to think of how a complete protein such as a chicken breast would fit in the palm of your hand. This will supply 30–40 percent protein as part of a meal—the right amount for an average person.

However, we all require slightly differing amounts of protein, and I have found that as much as 40–50 percent protein works for me; you may thrive on less—or perhaps more. Complex carbohydrates complete the meal, although vegetables must, without fail, make up at least 60 percent of these carbohydrates.

	MEAT & POULTRY
Ideal choice These foods are all complete proteins and are therefore the best protein choice.	Eggs, including chicken, duck, and quail Liver, including chicken, calves', and lambs' Skinless chicken and turkey Veal
Good choice You can include these food choices frequently as part of a healthy diet.	
Adequate choice Eat these foods occasionally.	Bacon Lamb chops Beef Pork chops Ham Ground beef

Why is fish so good for you?

Fish really does offer the best of both worlds. Not only is it an ideal source of protein, it is also rich in omega-3 essential fats. These fats have many functions in the body, but in terms of weight loss research has shown that such fats promote weight loss. Omega-3 fats also have an important role in promoting cardiovascular health, reducing the risk of Type 2 diabetes, and enhancing brain function.

DAIRY	VEGETARIAN	FISH			
	Chickpeas	Anchovy	Grey mullet*	Monkfish	Sprat*
	Lentils	Bluefish*	Haddock	Orange roughy	Swordfish*
	Nuts (raw)	Bream	Hake	Perch*	Tilapia
	Pumpkin seeds	Brill	Halibut*	Red mullet*	Trout*
	Quinoa	Carp*	Herring*	Salmon*	Tuna*
	Quorn	Cod	Lemon sole	Sardine*	Turbot
	Sesame seeds	Dover sole	Mackerel*	Sea bass	Whitebait*
	Sunflower seeds	Eel*	Mahi Mahi*	Sea bream	Whiting
	Tofu	Flounder	Marlin*	Skate	
Low-fat cottage cheese	Baked beans (unsweetened)				
Low-fat plain yogurt with active cultures					
Full-fat plain yogurt with active cultures					
Hard cheese			*Also a good source of omega-3 fats		

Carbohydrate profiles

	GRAIN-BASED FOODS		FRUITS	
Ideal choice The complex carbohydrates at this level are ideal choices because they supply high levels of energy for longer periods *(see p.48–49)*. They are all broken down slowly into glucose by the body so they have a low GI rating.	Barley Oatmeal Whole-grain rye bread		Apples Apricots (fresh) Blackberries Cranberries Grapefruit Lemons Limes Peaches	Pears Plums Strawberries
Good choice The foods in this category have a medium GI score and so they provide reasonably good levels of energy at a fairly steady rate.	Brown rice Couscous Granola bars containing nuts Pumpernickel bread Whole-wheat pasta and spaghetti Whole-grain bread		Blueberries Cherries Grapes Mangoes Oranges Papayas Peaches Pineapple Tangerines	
Adequate choice This category contains poor food choices. These carbohydrates are either refined, low in fiber, high in sugar or a combination of all three. As a result, they provide only short-term energy.	Bagels Biscuits Breadsticks Commercial breakfast cereals Cookies Couscous Croissants Doughnuts	French bread Melba toast Muffins White bread "White" pasta and spaghetti White rice	Bananas Dried fruit Dried nuts Figs Fruit juices Prunes Watermelon	

COOKED VEGETABLES		RAW FOODS	ALCOHOL
Artichokes	Greens	Bean and other sprouts	
Asparagus	String beans	Mushrooms	
Bok choy	Kale	Tomatoes	
Broccoli	Leeks	Various salad greens	
Brussels sprouts	Onions		
Cabbage	Peppers		
Cauliflower	Spinach		
Carrots		Avocado	
Kidney beans		Beets	
Pumpkin and other winter squash		Carrots	
Turnips		Celery root	
Zucchini		Olives	
Eggplant			Beer
Parsnips			Spirits
Peas			Wine
Potatoes (baked, boiled, mashed)			
Sweet potatoes			
Yams			

Principle 2
Stay hydrated

We all know how important it is to drink plenty of water, and it is common knowledge that to lose weight you must drink at least six glasses of water a day. Water is also the best thirst quencher; other beverages can only quench your thirst in proportion to the amount of water they contain.

There can be no doubt that keeping your fluid intake consistently high is imperative in order to aid weight loss. So does that mean drinking plain water only throughout the day? Many people ask me whether the water in tea, coffee, canned drinks, alcohol, juices, and soups can count toward this fluid intake.

Regular tea and coffee contain caffeine, which has a mild diuretic effect and reduces overall hydration. So these drinks do not count toward your required fluid intake. Canned drinks, most of which are carbonated and probably sugared, too, also don't count. Soups and juices do, but nothing beats water. Drink at least four glasses of water a day in addition to any other liquids.

Limit your alcohol intake

Alcohol can have a detrimental effect on any weight-loss plan. Alcohol is a fermented product and, as such can affect the levels of beneficial bacteria in the intestines (see pp.8–11). It's also defined as a simple sugar, so it affects glucose levels quite rapidly—added to which it also acts as a dehydrating element.

The final blow is that alcohol reduces your resolve. In other words, even if you are following all ten principles and succeeding in your weight-loss plan, after a glass of alcohol your thoughts may wander to sugary, fatty foods, which can undermine all your good efforts. Having said that, alcohol is a part of life, so there is a way to slot it into the Food Doctor plan. I suggest that you drink alcohol no more than three times a week and limit yourself to two glasses of wine or two measures of spirits without mixers, which are highly sweetened. If you have been used to drinking alcohol most evenings,

cutting down to a maximum of two or three times a week is an important first step. Wine is the best choice—although stay away from sweet wines—followed by pure vodka mixed with plenty of sparkling water, ice, and a squeeze of fresh lime juice. I do not recommend beers, stouts, lagers, or hard cider, all of which contain yeast, if not sugar, and can be detrimental to overall digestive health.

Avoid salt

Excess salt intake can contribute to thirst, and the most likely sources of salt in the modern diet are prepared foods. Since this weight-loss plan does not include such foods, your salt intake will automatically drop. Stop adding salt in cooking or to your food, and use herbs (either dried or fresh), freshly ground black pepper or sugar-free mustards to flavor foods instead.

ALCOHOL: THE GOLDEN RULES

1 Never drink alcohol on an empty stomach. Drinking alcohol with food is preferable, so have your first drink when you start your meal to reduce the absorption of alcohol.

2 Drink alcohol no more than three times a week—preferably less.

3 Mix spirits with water and ice, not mixers or fruit juices.

4 Do not drink alcohol on two consecutive nights.

Tap or bottled water?

With regard to weight loss, there is little difference between choosing tap, bottled mineral, or filtered water to drink as long as you drink at least four glasses of plain water a day in addition to juices and soups (totaling at least six glasses a day). This figure should be increased when you are exercising or during hot weather.

Still, rather than sparkling, bottled mineral water is my preferred choice as the gas that is contained in sparkling water can encourage bloating and discomfort.

Principle 3
Eat a wide variety of food

If you have a long-term weight issue, it's very possible that some foods have, over time, become off limits in your mind, while you have grown to consider other foods "safe." This often limits the range of foods you buy as you stick with only the ones that you feel most comfortable eating.

When I ask new clients to keep a food diary of their eating habits for a few days *(see pp.16–17)*, all too often I am struck by the fact that they eat the same food nearly every day. In fact, for 90 percent of the time most of us tend to buy the same small percentage—as little as 10 percent—of foods available to us. We invariably shop, select, and order food almost as if we are on autopilot, buying identical products week in, week out. Likewise, many weight-loss plans focus purely on a small group of foods. Perhaps in the past you have found that such dieting plans initially seem to work well when you eat the same food every day? Yet this strategy eventually makes any plan hard to follow, since you inevitably become bored and seek out foods from the so-called "forbidden list" that you know will satisfy you instead.

Why variety is important
It's vital to eat a wide variety of foods in order to benefit from the wonderful array of nutrients that food offers. And in order to encourage a healthy relationship with food, I suggest that you be brave and try one new food every week. Some of the ideal foods listed in the proteins and carbohydrates charts *(see pp.50–53)* may be new to you, in which case I hope you will try them. Similarly, although some of the ingredients listed in the recipe section *(see pp.104–37)* may not be familiar to you, please do try them, too.

So next time you are in the supermarket or at your local green market, buy something you have never tried before. You might want to flick through a cookbook first to look for something that appeals to you, or ask your shopkeeper how to cook what you have bought.

I am sure that once you begin to try a range of new foods, you will enjoy many of them and add them regularly to your usual shopping list, thus making the foods you eat more varied and interesting.

The issue of grains
You may have noticed that grain-based foods do not figure heavily in the Seven-Day Diet plan, nor do they appear much in the long-term Plan for Life. The reason is that some grains contain elements that can easily aggravate the sensitive lining of the digestive tract.

FOOD INTOLERANCE
There is much discussion these days about how many wheat and dairy products people should eat. While I do not think that avoiding either food is altogether necessary for everyone, there is a strong case for becoming aware of just how much of one food you might be eating and whether it is causing inflammation in your intestines *(see box, p.58)*. You may have a food intolerance if you suffer from any of the following symptoms:

- Bloating
- Diarrhea or constipation
- Dark circles under the eyes
- Excessive flatulence
- Runny nose
- Fatigue

Do you buy
the same food every week?

It's all too easy to become stuck in our shopping habits and repeatedly buy the same foods that we know and rely on. Ideally, however, we should all try to eat one new food a week, be it a vegetable, fruit, grain, legume, or herb. You will develop a taste for exciting new flavors and enjoy broadening your experience of foods.

Gluten grains

Wheat, rye, barley and oats are known as gluten grains because they all contain gliadin in varying amounts. Gliadin is a substance found in gluten grains that can irritate the lining of the intestinal tract. Gluten is a sticky substance that helps trap the air in bread, ensuring that it expands and has the correct feel. In recent years, grains have been cross-bred to produce new variants with a higher gluten content. If you look at the grain family tree *(see below),* you will notice that wheat, barley oats, and rye are closely related, and rice slightly less so, while corn, millet, and cane sugar are from the other side of the family.

Over the years, I have worked with many clients who have benefitted enormously from minimizing their intake of grains, especially those containing gluten. Having said that, grains are included in small amounts in both the Seven-Day Diet and the Plan for Life because they are good sources of fiber and are rich in B vitamins, both essential to weight loss. So do eat some wheat products, but keep the amounts as low as you can. Where possible, try to vary your grains. For example, buy 100 percent rye bread one week, yeast-free soda bread the next, and whole-grain brown bread the week after that.

Pasta, made from refined wheat, is often served and eaten in large quantities. If you want to eat pasta, have a few strands as part of a meal—much as you would have some potatoes or a scoop of rice. Avoid eating a whole bowl of pasta, even if it's just as an appetizer. When you shop buy wholewheat pasta, which is a complex carbohydrate, or try products made from corn or rice flour (a word of warning: They do not have the same consistency as wheat pasta and are more likely to be soft than *al dente*).

WHEAT AND WEIGHT PROBLEMS

There does seem to be a link between wheat intake and weight problems for some people. Wheat contains around 45 percent gliadin, the substance that can cause irritation and lead to the mild inflammation of the lining of the gut. If you think that wheat may be linked to any digestive problems you have, visit a nutritionist for advice. Even if you do not have a food intolerance, vary your intake of grains weekly.

THE RELATIONSHIP OF MAJOR CEREAL GRAINS

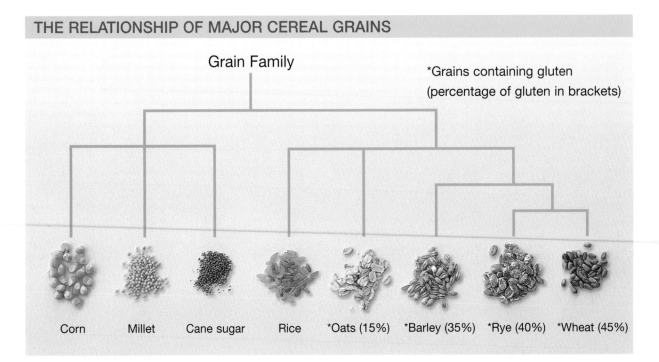

Grain Family

*Grains containing gluten (percentage of gluten in brackets)

Corn   Millet   Cane sugar   Rice   *Oats (15%)   *Barley (35%)   *Rye (40%)   *Wheat (45%)

How much dairy should I have?

Many diets exclude dairy products, but as my aim is to encourage you to eat a wide variety of foods, I suggest that you include dairy products from time to time. If you are concerned about the possibility of food intolerance from dairy products, goats' or sheeps' milk and cheese may be slightly more easy to tolerate than cows' milk or cheese, or try one of the many new lactose-free dairy products now available in most stores.

Principle 4
Fuel up frequently

You are probably becoming used to the idea that if you eat the right combination of foods that are broken down into glucose slowly, you will create a consistent supply of energy and still lose weight. But it's not just the food combinations and amounts that are important—it's the timing, too.

Eating little and often is a crucial element of the Plan for Life. By eating small meals and snacks at regular intervals through the day, you should be able to keep your energy levels constant so that you can function well without food cravings—the downfall of so many dieters.

The benefits explained

In the same way that you need to eat proteins with complex carbohydrates to maximize the benefits of a healthy diet and minimize the frequency of insulin production *(see p.12)*, so fueling up frequently ensures

ENERGY TIMELINE

The pink line on this energy timeline depicts the range of highs and lows that a typical person will experience through the day. Set against those peaks and valleys is the stabilizing green line of the Food Doctor plan, which illustrates how eating the right foods at certain times can help you avoid lows and keep energy levels constant.

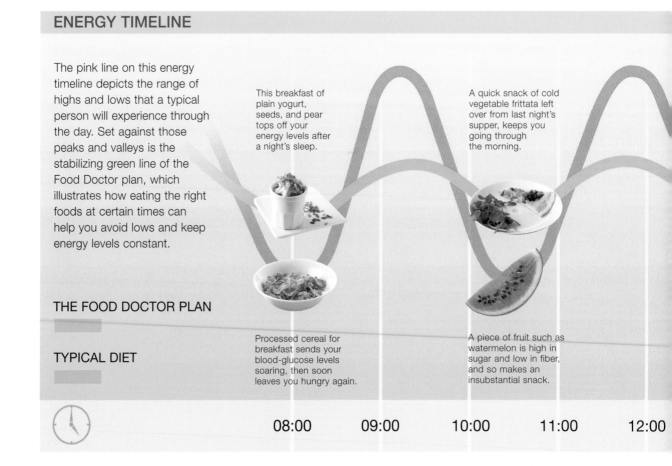

This breakfast of plain yogurt, seeds, and pear tops off your energy levels after a night's sleep.

A quick snack of cold vegetable frittata left over from last night's supper, keeps you going through the morning.

THE FOOD DOCTOR PLAN

TYPICAL DIET

Processed cereal for breakfast sends your blood-glucose levels soaring, then soon leaves you hungry again.

A piece of fruit such as watermelon is high in sugar and low in fiber, and so makes an insubstantial snack.

08:00   09:00   10:00   11:00   12:00

that a steady supply of glucose enters the bloodstream to be converted into energy. Together, these two factors create a potent mix of the right food at the right time, leading to effective weight loss and stable energy levels.

How it works in practice

Within two hours of eating breakfast, your blood-glucose levels begin to drop. These levels continue to diminish until they reach a low point that the body interprets as hunger. There is an optimal window of time just before you begin to feel the pangs of hunger, and it is during this time that eating something satisfying and healthy will make all the difference in your energy levels. This may mean that you have to teach yourself to recognize the first signs of hunger, which can take a number of forms ranging from loss of concentration to feeling slightly shaky. If you have

dieted previously, you will be familiar with the big midmorning dip depicted in the diagram below. If, however, you follow the Food Doctor plan and eat an appropriate snack *(see pp.82–83)* midway through the morning, you will be able to combat a slight dip in energy levels and any associated symptoms of hunger.

Ideally, you should be eat approximately every two or three hours through the day. So you need to include a proper lunch and another healthy snack in the middle of the afternoon before your evening meal.

Think of this principle as the equivalent of filling up your car with just enough premium-grade fuel to last you to the next filling station, and then doing the same again and again throughout the day. In this way you can combat hunger pangs and bad food choices, minimize insulin production, maximize your energy levels, and lose weight, all at the same time.

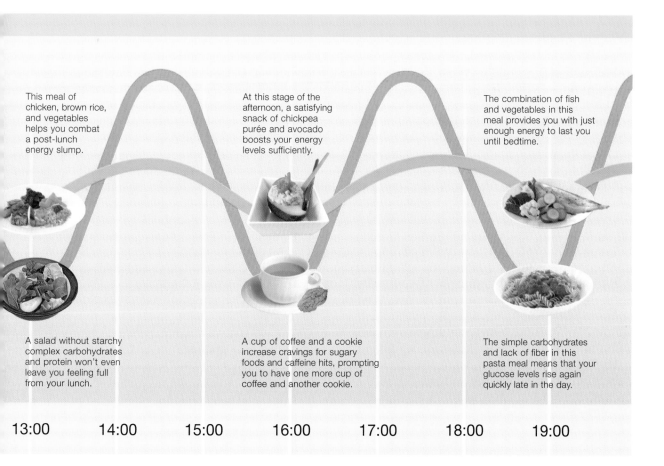

This meal of chicken, brown rice, and vegetables helps you combat a post-lunch energy slump.

At this stage of the afternoon, a satisfying snack of chickpea purée and avocado boosts your energy levels sufficiently.

The combination of fish and vegetables in this meal provides you with just enough energy to last you until bedtime.

A salad without starchy complex carbohydrates and protein won't even leave you feeling full from your lunch.

A cup of coffee and a cookie increase cravings for sugary foods and caffeine hits, prompting you to have one more cup of coffee and another cookie.

The simple carbohydrates and lack of fiber in this pasta meal means that your glucose levels rise again quickly late in the day.

13:00   14:00   15:00   16:00   17:00   18:00   19:00

Principle 5
Eat breakfast

Unlike many diets that leave you hungry and craving forbidden foods, this diet plan promotes eating little and often as the key to keeping your energy levels consistent and achieving successful weight loss. So it is essential that at the start of each day you eat a healthy breakfast.

Skipping any meal is one step to failure, and by far the worst meal to skip is breakfast. You may not have much of an appetite first thing and I appreciate that mornings can be stressful with kids to organize as well as getting yourself ready for work, but investing time in eating breakfast is fundamental to losing weight.

Time for a change
If you are the sort of person who has a cup of tea or coffee and a bowl of processed breakfast cereal to kick-start your day, then the time has come to make some changes to your diet.

Let's look at what this typical breakfast does to your body. The cereal almost certainly lacks protein. It is converted into glucose rapidly by the body, and so produces only short-term energy. Coupled with the caffeine, it may make you feel satisfied, but only for a short time. If you eat breakfast at 8am, by 10am it is likely that you will experience an energy slump, which is perceived as hunger. If you have another cup of coffee and a cookie or two, the whole cycle starts again. As the Plan for Life is designed to help you feel energetic and reduce hunger pangs, your intake of caffeinated drinks and sugary foods should be kept to a minimum.

A better approach
Eating the right foods little and often is the key to increased energy and sustained weight loss. If you eat a healthy breakfast, such as muesli or natural yogurt with fruit and seeds, you shouldn't feel hungry until 10.30–11am, which is the best time to eat a snack in order to sustain your energy levels. These types of

breakfasts are easy to prepare and have the right combination of food groups: the nuts, seeds, and yogurt provide your body with plenty of protein and the wholegrains are rich in complex carbohydrates. If you do not enjoy yogurt or muesli, there are many other healthy options for breakfast, including eggs, toast, crackers, fruit, and smoothies. See pages 78–79 for a range of suggestions to inspire you. Whatever you decide to eat, remember that taking a few minutes to eat a good breakfast is essential and sets the scene for the rest of the day.

CAN I HAVE COFFEE?

I love coffee and I feel that no morning is complete without it. As long as you have coffee with or after a meal or snack containing protein and fiber, you should be able to keep your energy levels high. However, do not have more than one or two cups a day because caffeine stimulates your adrenal glands to produce adrenaline. This is the same response your body has under stress, and is part of what is known as the "flight or fight" response—providing short-term energy, a heightened sense of sight, and hearing and quickened responses. Once the "danger" has passed, adrenaline production stops, energy levels reduce and you may experience fatigue and hunger, which in turn encourages you to make poor food choices. Try to limit yourself to one cup a day, and don't add sugar to your drink. By now your sugar cravings should be manageable, so it shouldn't be too hard.

Is your breakfast really balanced?

My preferred choice of milk

I suggest that you buy full-fat milk for your breakfasts and drinks instead of skimmed milk. There isn't much difference between the two in terms of fat, yet skimmed and semi-skimmed milk are higher in sugars that full-fat milk, and so will affect your sugar intake.

The ideal muesli

Choose a muesli that contains plenty of nuts and seeds and not too much dried fruit, since this combination will be broken down into glucose relatively slowly. Or, rather than buying ready-made muesli, why not visit your local health-food store and buy the ingredients separately to make up your own muesli mix *(see box, left)*?

Principle 6
Avoid sugar

I believe that sugar is just as much to blame for weight gain as is fat. You will benefit enormously by cutting down on the amount of sugar in your diet and, since the Food Doctor plan is designed to help you achieve good digestive health, avoiding sugar takes on added importance.

It is worth explaining exactly what I mean by the word *sugar*. There are many variations on the white or brown granules that you buy in packets, including sorbitol, malt, and even honey (*see box, below*). With so many different names for sugar, it is no wonder that most people have little idea just how much of it may be present in their diet.

By limiting your sugar intake, you will reduce the amount and frequency of insulin secretion in the body. Sugar in all its forms has very few bonds holding it together, so the digestive system breaks it down into glucose extremely quickly. As the blood-glucose levels suddenly rise high, they trigger the production of insulin (*see p.12*), which in turn forces the glucose levels down again by converting the glucose into fat through a series of biochemical changes—hence the reason why

we need to minimize insulin production if we want to lose weight. Food that is converted into glucose rapidly should be avoided or, at the very least, combined with foods that are broken down slowly.

The fat-free myth
Sugars of one kind or another are almost always added to processed and ready-made foods, and it's not uncommon for a product to contain several different types of sugar. The more sugar there is in a product, the less fat it contains, which allows manufacturers to claim that it is low in fat or that it contains less than a certain percentage of fat. In reality, this means that in your desire to lose weight you buy, for example, a product that is labeled 95 percent fat free. You have probably done so for years. So why don't you become the thin person you want to be when all you eat is this type of food? The answer is that the sugars in these products are always higher when the fat content has been decreased.

How the theory works
Let's see how this theory works in practice. You choose a low-fat muffin for breakfast or a snack (*see right*). As its sugar content is higher than that of a regular muffin your blood-sugar levels rise sharply and then fall quickly, leaving you hungry again all too soon. You battle with your food cravings, give in, and eat another low-fat snack.

If you eat a meal or snack containing complete protein and complex carbohydrate (*see pp.62–63*), the insulin produced is minimal by comparison and your prolonged energy levels and reduced hunger pangs even enable you to make sensible choices about what to eat next.

ALTERNATIVE NAMES FOR SUGAR

Although these substances are derived from a variety of sources, they are all classed as sugars.

- Corn syrup
- Fructose
- Glucose
- Honey
- Invert sugar
- Lactose
- Malt
- Malt extract
- Maltose
- Mannitol
- Maple syrup
- Molasses
- Rice extract
- Rice syrup
- Sorbitol
- Sucrose

Can I use artificial sweeteners instead?

Sweeteners are usually added to so-called diet drinks and processed foods. In the Food Doctor plan you won't be eating any of these foods, so the issue of sweeteners will not come up. If you add sweeteners to your coffee and tea, try to stop. Sweeteners have no nutritional value and can affect the overall benefits of the Plan for Life by perpetuating any cravings you may have for sweet foods.

Which is the best option?

If you choose to eat a low-fat muffin, its calorie count may be low—but check its sugar content against a regular muffin. The low-fat muffin almost certainly contains a higher percentage of sugars, and thus it is a simple carbohydrate that the body can convert from food to glucose with ease. As a result, blood-glucose levels rise and insulin is released, which in turn increases fat stores in the body.

Full-fat cranberry muffin

Full-fat muffins consist of refined white flour, sugar, and fat. Fruits, such as cranberries, and fiber, such as bran, supply only a small amount of complex carbohydrates.

simple carbohydrates 80%
of which sugar 40%, white flour 40%

complex carbohydrates 5%

vegetable fat 15%

Low-fat cranberry muffin

This low-fat muffin may contain less saturated fat, but to compensate more sugar has been added during the manufacturing process.

simple carbohydrates 90%
of which sugar 60%, white flour 40%

complex carbohydrates 5%

vegetable fat 5%

Principle 7
Exercise is essential

A weight-loss program will not be successful if you do not exercise, just as exercising frequently while eating the wrong foods isn't likely to result in a healthier lifestyle. Even in the busiest lives, there is time to do more if you want to, so make exercise a priority.

My expertise is in food, not in exercise, but I do know that the benefits of exercising are far reaching, and not just in the area of weight loss. Regular exercise can help reduce the risk of cardiovascular disease, osteoporosis, and Type 2 diabetes. Exercise can even help you cope with stress more effectively.

Adjusting your metabolic rate
Exercise increases your metabolic rate, that is, the speed at which your body uses up food as energy. Likewise, the idea of exercise in the context of the Food Doctor plan is to increase the rate at which the food you eat, and any stores of fat, are utilized for energy.

Remember that this eating plan relies on supplying premium-grade fuel, in the form of whole foods, to the body, where it is converted into glucose and circulated in the blood to cells to be used as fuel for energy production. On my Plan for Life, the rate of glucose entering the cells is steady enough to keep energy levels consistent and avoid lows (which we interpret as hunger).

However, it is possible to influence how that glucose, or fuel, is managed at cellular level. In each cell there is a tiny power plant, called a mitochondria, which effectively converts the glucose into energy. Cells are amazingly advanced structures that respond to the body's requirements, so if you increase your energy output, the cells respond accordingly by creating more of these tiny mitochondria in each cell to make yet more energy. Thus you can affect how much glucose is used up as energy. Exercising encourages this smooth conversion of glucose into energy because consistent and increased energy helps your body burn off that unwanted fat.

What sort of exercise is best?
I am a firm believer that you should always consult an appropriate professional if you need advice about what type of exercise to undertake. I wouldn't suggest taking nutritional advice from an instructor unless he or she is also a trained nutritionist, and since I am not an exercise expert I only make suggestions as to what might suit you.

If you decide to join a gym, ask a trained instructor to help you devise a simple routine that you can stick to and enjoy, since I have found that, even with the best intentions, the gym can become boring after a while. Try to vary your exercise routine, or exercise with a friend who has goals similar to your own. This makes it more fun, and you can chat as you work out.

Depending on your current level of fitness, you could try jogging, swimming, hiking, biking, walking the dog or playing soccer, tennis, or squash. The list of possibilities is endless.

If the thought of exercising is abhorrent to you, then start off gently. Try walking to your local stores every other day instead of driving, or getting off the bus or train a stop early on the way to work and walking briskly the rest of the way. As long as you exercise for a minimum of 30 minutes, three times a week, the exercise you choose is not that important. You needn't punish yourself in the gym: Instead you should raise your heartbeat to a level at which you break out in a sweat at some point over the half hour, while still being able to continue a conversation.

So, be creative with your choice of exercise. The benefits are many and your progress with the Food Doctor plan will be greatly enhanced.

What to eat after exercise?

You may well find that you feel hungrier if you are exercising regularly. Increase your portion sizes a little at mealtimes to match this, but by no more than ten percent. You should also make sure that you have appropriate snacks to eat immediately after you have exercised. It is especially important to replenish spent glucose levels after any exercise, so eat something that contains complex carbohydrates as well as protein, such as a cereal bar that contains oats, fruit, nuts, and seeds.

Which type of exercise?

The bottom line is that you must be physically active, be it swimming, jogging, playing tennis, dancing, going to the gym, or simply walking. Try to complete at least 30 minutes of exercise in any form three times a week or more. This will help raise your metabolic rate and improve your overall digestion, helping you to get rid of any excess fat stores that you have accumulated.

Principle 8
Follow the 80:20 rule

Perhaps you have followed diets in the past that revolve around sticking to the prescribed plan 100 percent of the time. The problem is that it is in our nature to veer off course after a while— usually out of frustration or boredom—hence, the all-important 80:20 rule.

The Food Doctor plan encourages you to eat little and often so that your hunger pangs are minimized and you are unlikely to suffer from food cravings.

However, life just isn't that easy, as we all know, and from time to time you will stray from the plan. I know that however many practical suggestions for coping with special occasions, interesting recipes, or sound advice this book contains, there will be times when nothing will work for you apart from your chosen treat, be it chocolate cake, candy, or ice cream. The good news is that this is entirely possible, within reason.

Putting the rule into practice

So what constitutes the 80:20 rule? If you follow the Plan for Life principles—such as combining the right food groups and avoiding refined carbohydrates and sugars— as closely as possible, then I believe that your food will satisfy you and your success rate will be high. By eating

regularly to keep blood-glucose levels up, you won't want to eat the types of foods that you probably see as treats now. Yet the experience of eating goes further than just supplying energy. Follow the plan for 80 percent of the time and you will still achieve success, albeit more slowly. For example, if you eat healthfully through the day, you can save your 20 percent for when you are out to dinner or at a party. There is more information about this in the section on special situations (see pp.92–95).

Try not to veer from the the Food Doctor plan every day—that could create a habit in which you crave the wrong types of food. As a consequence, following the Plan for Life will become harder to do and the possibility of slipping back into old habits increases. On average, use the 80:20 rule to treat yourself two or three times a week, perhaps taking into account any situations you have coming up where you may not be able to eat what you would ideally choose.

EATING OUT

When you have a choice about where to eat, stick to a restaurant or café that you know will enable you to eat in line with the Plan for Life principles. It's possible to eat well nearly everywhere as long as you keep food proportions in your mind when ordering. For example, have a vegetable-based starter without pastry and a complete protein for the main course. If you have no choice as to the venue, then hopefully you can allocate your 20 per cent quota to this meal. If not, then eat as carefully as you can and make up for it later.

What can I do about chocolate?

Chocolate tends to be by far the one food that is craved more than any other, and it can be the downfall of so many dieters. Here are some guidelines to follow:

- The pleasure in eating chocolate should come from the flavor of the bean, not from the fats and sugar that make up around 80 percent of more popular brands.

- If you crave chocolate, eat a couple of squares of the richest, darkest variety you can find—preferably one that contains more than 70 percent cocoa. The higher the bean content, the lower the sugar and fat content. Two squares of dark chocolate are far more satisfying than lesser varieties.

- If you are the sort of person who can't eat just two squares of chocolate, try breaking the bar into small chunks and putting the rest safely away for another time.

Principle 9
Make time to eat

Eating is an essential yet pleasurable social ritual, and one that I feel has become devalued in our society. Fast food, ready-made meals, and the pressure we all impose on ourselves to save time have eliminated the importance of sitting down to enjoy a meal. So make time to eat!

I have had consultations with many clients who, while they are accountable in other areas of their lives as—parents or employees, for example—seem to take no interest in or responsibility for what they eat. Ironically, some of these clients will change their eating habits if they find that they are pregnant, or planning a pregnancy, only to change back again after their baby is born. This is often in spite of feeling much better on the healthier pregnancy eating plan.

I have also worked with many families who rush through dinner, both cooking and eating their meal simply so that they can spend the rest of the evening in front of the television watching cooking shows!

Modern life seems to have taken the pleasure out of cooking and eating food. It seems to be something that is not worth fussing over, and it wastes valuable time. The message is: Let the food manufacturers do your work for you so that you can do something more important instead. If this lifestyle sounds familiar to you, then ask yourself how prepared and processed foods have contributed to your weight problems. If you learn to value and respect good food, making time to eat will become normal practice for you and your family. Try to sit down and eat at least one meal a day together. Take your time eating, and you may even find that you linger at the table chatting after your meal is over.

Eating at work
If your job is stressful and you never get a chance to eat a real meal, you will probably snack when you can and rush through a sandwich at lunchtime. However, on the Food Doctor plan I want you to eat little and often, and this means eating midmorning and midafternoon snacks that may require you to leave your desk and take a few minutes to prepare and eat them (see pp.82–83). You may need to plan ahead in the early stages until you become used to the plan, but the snack doesn't have to be complicated or take more than a minute to prepare. More importantly, taking the time to eat properly and chew well will ensure that you supply yourself with enough energy to see you through until your next meal.

If you really cannot leave your desk, keep a bag of raw, unsalted nuts in your drawer and measure a palmful of them in your hand to eat with an apple. If you have appointments or meetings throughout the day, try to leave a gap of a few minutes between them so that you can eat. If you don't, you are more likely to rely on coffee and cookies and then make a poor food choice at lunchtime because your energy levels will be low and need to be replenished quickly.

THE BENEFITS OF TAKING TIME TO EAT

- Your levels of stress are reduced.
- Chewing slowly and thoroughly enables you to digest your food properly and maintain good digestive health.
- Your body can absorb the nutrients from your food more effectively.
- You will have a feeling of satisfaction from having eaten a tasty, filling meal.

Why should I stop to eat at work?

Try to view eating your lunch or snack at work as a separate activity that you should concentrate on—don't treat it as a distraction or an afterthought. You must take the time to eat slowly and digest your food properly, so move away from your desk or computer screen while you eat.

Principle 10
Eat fat to lose fat

If you come from a background of calorie counting, you probably see fat as the enemy. Yet although the fat accumulated in our bodies and the fats in food are, in theory, similar, they are actually quite different: The essential fats present in a variety of foods are crucial for the body to function properly.

Fat contains nine calories per gram, the highest calorie count of any food there is, and this is why many diet plans advocate limiting your intake of fatty foods. However, I believe that it is saturated fats, not the all-important essential fats, that should be avoided.

What's the difference?
There are many types of fats that the body uses in a variety of different ways. Some fats are termed essential, as they must come from the food we eat *(see right)*. The conversion of these essential fats into substances that can be used by our bodies is dependent upon several enzymes, which themselves require specific nutrients in order to work efficiently. Even those fats that are nonessential to the body have a role to play, although saturated fats are not required in any great amount. Furthermore, fat adds to the satisfaction of eating—

known in the food industry as "mouth feel"—and is considered a vital part of the eating experience. When we eat fat, a substance called galanin that actually increases our desire to eat more fat is released into the body. This is why we often crave fatty foods, and why they are so pleasurable to eat. Luckily, this same feeling is experienced when we eat essential fats, which should form the bulk of our fat intake.

How much is too much?
Research has shown that a diet supplying not more than 30 percent of energy from fat is the best way to lose weight. So you will find that by including 20 percent of fat in the form of essential fats in your diet, you will still enjoy the satisfaction of eating, yet the rate at which your food is converted into glucose is slowed down, thus fitting in perfectly with the Plan for Life principles.

FOOD LABELS

If you buy, for example, a packet of potato or corn chips that claims to be low in fat, you may see something like "less than five percent fat" advertised on the front of the package. The food label *(see top right)* also lists the product as being only 22 percent fat, but this does not take into account the number of calories you will eat from fat. Fat contains nine calories per gram, and the total calorie count of this product is 470 calories. The fat, by weight, on the label

	Per 100g
Energy	470 calories
Protein	7.5 g
Carbohydrates	60.0 g
of which sugars	0.5g
Fats	22.0g

	Per 100g
Energy	470 calories
Protein	49 calories of total
Fats	198 calories
Calories from fat	42%

comprises 22 grams. But that can be misleading. When you eat the chips, you must multiply 22 grams by nine calories to determine how much energy this food supplies, which in this case is 198. While shopping, look for calories from fat in nutritional information listed on packages and calculate the percentage yourself by multiplying the number of grams of fat by nine. In this example *(see bottom left)*, although the total number of calories is 470, the number of calories from fat is actually 42 percent, not 22 percent.

Which fats are good?

Foods that contain essential fats

Overall, the fats that are naturally found in fish (such as salmon, mackerel, tuna, trout, eel, and sardines), raw nuts, seeds, and olives are those that are most beneficial to your diet. However, don't go overboard with these foods; be aware of how much you are eating, and aim to eat no more than a handful of nuts daily and fish four or five times a week.

Which oils are best?

The foods illustrated below all provide valuable essential fats in their most natural form. However, the oils derived from these foods are also beneficial in small quantities. Choose cold-pressed good-quality oils as the basis for salad dressings and marinades, and avoid cooking with these oils at high temperatures, as this causes them to lose nutritional value.

Avocado

Pumpkin

Sesame

Olive

Walnut

Hazelnut

Sunflower

Planning meals

This part of the book explains the practice behind the theory of the Plan for Life principles. Within this section are spreads to remind you of the main goals for each mealtime—what you should be eating and when—in order to sustain your energy levels and maintain a healthy digestive system. To help you remember the food groups in the Food Doctor plan, which consist of complete protein, starchy complex carbohydrates, and complex carbohydrates in the form of vegetables, each of these spreads carries my equation. These equations will help you think carefully about which categories your food choices fall into and to decide whether they are healthy enough to be part of this eating plan.

Deciding what to eat

The selections of suggested meal and snack options that follow on each of these spreads will provide a springboard to encourage you to think for yourself when deciding what to eat at each meal. These suggestions combine the food groups in the ratios that I feel are ideal for maximizing energy, reducing hunger, and promoting weight loss. Feel free to substitute any protein for another according to your preferences, and always include vegetables at lunch and dinner and with snacks to ensure that you don't end up eating a very high-protein diet.

Eating a **protein-rich** breakfast will supply you with **consistent fuel** to keep you going and feeling satisfied

Breakfast

We have already examined the principle of eating breakfast and how it sets the stage for rest of the day (see pp.62–63), but let's look more closely at how this theory works and why it is such a fundamental and important principle to establish.

The food you eat is broken down by the digestive system into component parts—glucose, vitamins, minerals, and so on. It is glucose that creates energy and acts as the fuel for every cell, so the food you eat at breakfast is responsible for providing you with energy for a significant part of the morning. In order to lose weight, you must eat the right ratio of food groups (see p.48) to ensure that glucose is released gradually into the bloodstream. This steady release, in turn, limits the production of insulin, which must be minimized for body fat to be reduced accordingly.

What is a healthy breakfast?

Having established that breakfast must include some foods that are broken down slowly by the body, the reality is that conventional breakfast foods are usually caffeine and simple carbohydrates, which supply a quick energy surge and little more. The image of a "healthy" breakfast of cereal, toast, orange juice, and black coffee is, in fact, based on the theory of calorie counting and does not include any protein. I can almost guarantee that this sort of typical breakfast will not meet your energy requirements for the morning, and as the glucose created from this food runs out, your body interprets this signal as hunger and you begin a cycle of desire and denial.

Eating a protein-rich breakfast will supply you with consistent fuel to keep you feeling satisfied so that you don't become overly hungry. Remember that this is a protein-*rich* breakfast, not a pure-protein one, so include some complex carbohydrates, too. This meal isn't always as instant as a bowl of cereal, so turn to pages 78–79 for some ideas, then set aside a few extra minutes each day to make a truly healthy breakfast.

THE FOOD DOCTOR BREAKFAST EQUATION

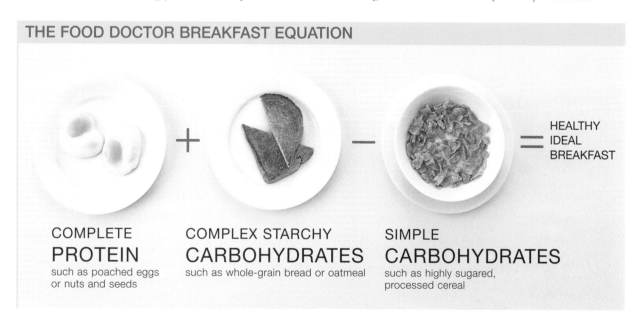

COMPLETE PROTEIN
such as poached eggs or nuts and seeds

+

COMPLEX STARCHY CARBOHYDRATES
such as whole-grain bread or oatmeal

−

SIMPLE CARBOHYDRATES
such as highly sugared, processed cereal

=

HEALTHY IDEAL BREAKFAST

Breakfast suggestions

Many of us tend to view breakfast as a time-consuming event that keeps us from starting the day, but it is important to remember that this meal is vital if you want to maintain high energy levels through the morning. These suggestions are easy to prepare, yet taste good and feel satisfying.

By now you should be familiar with the principle that protein combined with complex carbohydrates will provide a healthy, energy-giving meal (see pp.46–49). This is a crucial requirement for the first meal of the day. For example, if you have some fish left over from the night before and you want to eat it for breakfast, there is nothing to say that you shouldn't have it. It's not a typical choice, perhaps, but it fits in with the Food Doctor plan. You must eat some complex carbohydrates too, so you could either have a mouthful or two of vegetables, a couple of rice crackers, or a piece of rye toast.

Here are some suggestions to try that are simple yet may not be quite what you are used to.

Hot breakfasts

Two eggs scrambled, poached, or soft-boiled with a slice of rye toast or rice crackers

Eggs supply the protein in this meal, while the toast provides the complex carbohydrates. If you would like to try poached eggs with grilled tomatoes and mushrooms, turn to the recipe section (see p.108). If you don't have time to cook eggs in your preferred style in the morning, boil some eggs the night before and let them cool. At breakfast time, chop up the hard-boiled eggs, add chopped fresh herbs such as dill or tarragon, and eat the eggs with a piece of toast or rice crackers.

Oatmeal

A sustaining meal of oatmeal will provide you with some of the necessary fiber required for a healthy digestive system. Add protein in the form of a spoonful of plain yogurt or flaked almonds, and mix in some chopped pear to provide your complex carbohydrates (this also adds flavor)—or try an easy recipe for hot apple oats (see p.106).

Fish with grilled or steamed vegetables, or a piece of rye or whole-grain toast

Fish is delicious as well as quick and simple to cook and provides your body with valuable nutrients at the start of the day. Turn to the recipe section if you would like to try a poached-fish recipe (see p.109).

Uncooked breakfasts

Sugar-free cereal, such as flaked corn, with sunflower seeds

When you shop for a packaged cereal, check the ingredient label first to ensure that it does not contain any sugar. If you combine a serving of the cereal with a few hazelnuts and sunflower seeds, topped with a tablespoon of plain yogurt and a teaspoon of golden raisins, the cereal and raisins will provide your complex carbohydrates and the nuts, seeds, and yogurt will supply your protein.

Nut and seed muesli

A simple recipe to mix up your own muesli (see p.62) should be one that includes grains, nuts, and seeds to provide an ideal combination of the food groups. It may be worth making

BENEFICIAL NUTRIENTS

The best way to maximize your nutritional benefits from food is to eat as many unprocessed foods as possible. This is because the nutrient levels of whole grains remain intact because the grains have not been refined in any way. In contrast, the grains in processed cereals have been refined to such a degree that nutrient levels are depleted.

So when deciding what to eat for breakfast, remember that the fiber content and level of B vitamins in whole grains such as oats are potentially higher than those in processed cereals. In fact, oats contain most of the B vitamins, which have numerous functions in the body. These include being involved in the production of energy and in helping to maintain stable moods— which can, in turn, help to reduce cravings for sugar and caffeine.

up a quantity of muesli in advance and storing it in a sealed plastic container, ready for those mornings when you don't feel like doing anything more than pouring your breakfast into a bowl, adding some milk, and eating it immediately.

Plain yogurt with apple

For a tasty, quick breakfast, try mixing one chopped apple with two tablespoons of plain yogurt and sprinkle over a tablespoon of flaked almonds and pumpkin or sesame seeds. The yogurt, nuts, and seeds provide the protein while the apple provides the complex carbohydrate and fiber. Turn to the recipe section for a similar recipe that includes fresh pear (*see p.107*).

Tofu smoothie

Try a smoothie for a change. Use a food processor to blend 2oz (50g) of soft tofu, one chopped apple, and a tablespoon of either sunflower, pumpkin, or sesame seeds with your preferred choice of milk—cow's, goat, sheep's, rice or soy milk. Add a couple of drops of vanilla extract or one teaspoon of unsweetened cocoa powder if you wish, blend for a few seconds more, then drink.

Try a **refreshing smoothie,** made with **tofu, fruit, and seeds,** for a perfectly balanced breakfast

Ideally, you need to **eat** something almost **before** you **feel hungry** so that you **fuel up** just before your **glucose** levels dip **too low**

Snacks

By the middle of the morning or afternoon, the energy created from your last protein-rich meal will have been used up by your body for various functions—everything from breathing and thinking to walking and exercising. At this point, it is time to refuel again.

Assuming that you ate your breakfast at about 8:00AM, you should eat a midmorning snack between 10:30AM and 11:00AM. Likewise, if you ate lunch at one, have a snack at about four. Ideally, you should eat something almost before you feel hungry, so that you fuel up just before your glucose levels dip too low; don't wait until you feel ravenous.

Which snacks are best?

The snacks you choose needn't be a time-consuming culinary feast. For example, when I suggest eating some crudités and a dip, don't assume that you must cut the vegetables perfectly and arrange them artistically on a plate with the dip in the center. You can just as easily stand in the kitchen area, dip a carrot into an opened tub of dip, and munch it. After all, it's the combination of the complex carbohydrate and protein that is important, not how it is presented. However you decide to eat your snack, remember not to rush it and to chew each mouthful well.

If you go out to work, try to plan ahead by taking something simple with you in your bag, such as chopped raw vegetables and a few cubes of hard cheese. You only need to eat a few mouthfuls to make a satisfying snack.

Energy bars and drinks

Energy bars are not an ideal option. Many are advertised as "healthy," but they are not as wholesome as they seem. Look at the labels of energy bars or drinks and you will see that they all contain sugar in varying amounts. Also check whether the protein content is anywhere near the Food Doctor ratio of 40 percent. Ideally, opt for the suggested snacks on the next two pages.

THE FOOD DOCTOR SNACK EQUATION

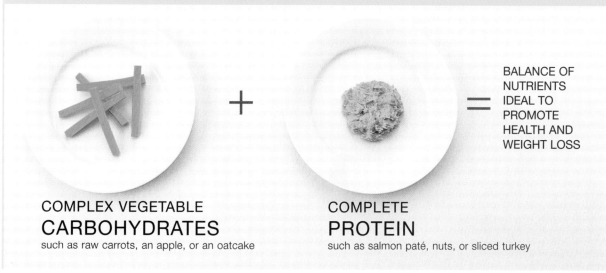

COMPLEX VEGETABLE
CARBOHYDRATES
such as raw carrots, an apple, or an oatcake

COMPLETE
PROTEIN
such as salmon paté, nuts, or sliced turkey

BALANCE OF NUTRIENTS IDEAL TO PROMOTE HEALTH AND WEIGHT LOSS

Snack suggestions

Snacking is an important element of the Plan for Life, and every midmorning and midafternoon snack must include a combination of the right food groups (as the equation on the previous page shows). The timing of each snack is also significant, as are the amounts you eat.

If you are careful not to leave too long a gap between your previous meal and your next snack, the chances are that you won't be tempted to overeat or make poor choices about what your snack should consist of.

Snacks should be easy and quick to prepare, although you may sometimes have to be a little creative with your ingredients. Take a piece of fruit and a package of mixed seeds or nuts in your bag—an apple and five nuts should make an ample snack. Even if you don't feel adventurous about what to eat, make sure that your snack is healthy and simple to make, that it consists of the correct proportion of protein and complex carbohydrates, and that it is something that you enjoy eating.

Easy options

A piece of fruit with raw nuts
Choose an apple or a pear to eat with five or six Brazil nuts or almonds. Nuts make an excellent standby, as you can buy small packages to keep at home or in your bag, briefcase, or backpack. It is important that you do not eat too many nuts—limit yourself to an average of five or six a day—and that you eat some carbohydrate, such as a piece of fruit, at the same time. You may prefer to substitute nuts with a handful of mixed sesame, pumpkin, and sunflower seeds.

Soy nuts are widely available and make an excellent high-protein alternative to other nuts as they contain far less fat. They may also be a good choice if you're looking for some variety.

Nut butter on two rice cakes, melba toasts, or a small piece of rye bread
Nut butters, such as peanut, cashew, or almond butter, are another good standby, but make sure that the products you buy are free of sugar and that you don't eat too much at once. A thin scraping of your choice of nut butter on a rice cake or piece of rye bread should suffice.

A tablespoon of dip with a few raw vegetables
Choose a dip such as guacamole, tzatziki, or hummus. See page 26 for a recipe if you would like to make your own hummus. Chop up a raw vegetable, such as a carrot, a rib of celery, some Belgian endive, cucumber, a few broccoli florets, or green beans, and use to to scoop up the dip and eat it. If you work, make things even easier for yourself by chopping up the vegetables at home first and storing the pieces in a plastic bag. Keep the bag in a refrigerator at work if you can.

Guacamole on two melba toasts or rye crispbread
See page 134 for an easy recipe for homemade guacamole. If you add lemon juice to the mixture when you make the dip, it will keep well in the refrigerator for up to 24 hours.

TAKING SUPPLEMENTS

Although supplements can play a significant role in maintaining our health, I feel that many of us take too many of these products without knowing exactly what they do or how they interact. Since the Plan for Life is designed to enhance your digestion and improve the absorption of nutrients, I would prefer that your vitamins and minerals come directly from your food intake. There are one or two supplements that might make a small difference to your well-being, but most of your success will come from your dietary and lifestyle changes, not from a bottle of pills. Rather than waste money on unnecessary supplements, make a one-time appointment with a nutritionist, who will be able to tell you which supplements, if any, will suit your requirements.

Assemblies

Choose any **one** of the following carbohydrate bases:

1 piece of rye toast or bread
2 melba toasts
2 rice cakes
2 corn cakes

Top it with your choice of any one of the following protein sources:

Cheese—any type, although cottage cheese is the best choicet. Avoid blue or aged cheeses.

Fish—a paté or spread made with any oily fish, such as mackerel, salmon, tuna, or sardine.

Eggs—a chopped hard-boiled egg combined with finely chopped herbs such as parsley, dill, or tarragon.

Chicken or turkey slices—use skinless poultry. If the meat comes from a deli or grocery store, ensure that it is sugar-free.

If you open your **hands** and **hold your palms** together, the **surface area** you see is the sort of **plate size** I have in mind

Lunch

When it comes to lunch, knowing that you need a good combination of complete protein, complex carbohydrates, and fiber is almost all the story, but not quite. This meal differs from your other meals in that you need to eat slightly larger quantities of food than you would at breakfast or dinner.

Your midmorning snack should have kept your glucose levels even until lunchtime, so around 1:00PM it will be time to fuel up again. For this meal, the quantities differ and you should eat a little more, although it is just as important that you do not overeat.

How much do I eat?

If you hold out one hand and open your palm, the portion of protein you should eat for lunch is a little smaller than the size of your palm. The remaining 60 percent of the food on your plate is made up of complex carbohydrates. If you then open

both hands and hold your palms together with your thumbs pulled in tightly to your forefingers, the surface area you see is the sort of plate size I have in mind. As long as your food isn't piled too high, you should be eating more or less the right amount of food.

If you have the time and you enjoy cooking, then by all means make the effort to prepare your food; given that digestive enzymes respond to visual stimuli, this process can help aid digestion. However, lunch doesn't have to be a beautifully prepared meal: You can easily cook a chicken

breast, or bring a cold, cooked piece of chicken in to work from home, and add a small jacket potato and vegetables or some brown rice salad. Not quite the visual feast you might hope for, but it can taste just as good and supply all the energy and nutrients you need through much of the afternoon.

If you usually buy sandwiches, I suggest that you buy sandwiches for only two days each week and prepare some homemade lunches for the other days. Turn to the following pages for some lunch suggestions to eat at home, at work, and on the go.

THE FOOD DOCTOR LUNCH EQUATION

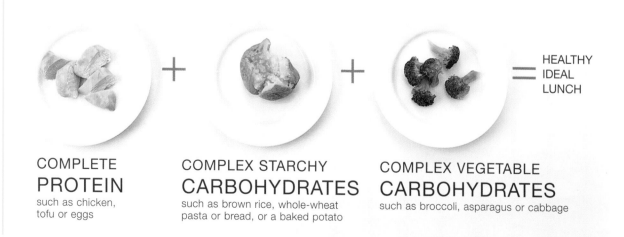

COMPLETE PROTEIN
such as chicken, tofu or eggs

COMPLEX STARCHY CARBOHYDRATES
such as brown rice, whole-wheat pasta or bread, or a baked potato

COMPLEX VEGETABLE CARBOHYDRATES
such as broccoli, asparagus or cabbage

= HEALTHY IDEAL LUNCH

Lunch suggestions

Lunch is often a rushed and merely functional meal, especially if you are working or busy with your day. Yet however little time you have, it is vital that you put aside ten minutes or so to relax and eat your lunch calmly and slowly.

Taking just a short amount of time to eat your lunch properly and chew your food well will help improve the process of digestion, thus allowing you to derive the maximum benefit from the good food you are eating. It also helps you to reduce your stress levels in the middle of a busy day.

Away from home

For many people, lunch is the one meal of the day that is eaten away from home, and if you make your own lunch you may want to organize in advance what you will eat to make sure that your meals fit in with the Plan for Life program. You might prefer to plan for the whole week, writing down a rough idea of what you intend to eat each lunchtime. You might want to tie in your plan with something you are going to make for your evening meal so that you can make extra quantities to take into work the following day. Here are some simple ideas to give you inspiration at lunchtime.

Meal options

One small baked potato
Add a portion of salmon, canned or fresh tuna fish, sardines, chicken, or beans to provide the protein, and serve with a large mixed salad.

One grilled turkey breast, tuna fillet, or a hard-boiled egg
Include a large salad that contains lettuce and at least five vegetables

Chickpeas and sliced red pepper
Add pine nuts, a green salad, and a salad dressing (see p.117).

Salade niçoise
Include your choice of tuna, black olives, and green beans (see p.116).

Chicken Caesar salad
Mix pieces of cold, grilled chicken breast with a large green salad and a dressing (see p.117).

Goat cheese salad
Mix the cheese with a large mixed salad and a dressing (see p.117).

Smoked mackerel fillet
Serve cold with a large green salad and half an avocado, sliced.

Mixed vegetable chowder
Using the recipe on page 124, substitute some diced fresh vegetables for the fish and seafood.

Fresh soup with rye or soda bread
Use lentils or beans and vegetables, or refer to the recipes on pages 23 and 123. Pea-and-ham or chicken-and-vegetable soup makes a well-balanced meal in a bowl.

Mixed lettuce salad
Add sliced turkey, fresh asparagus, and feta cheese.

Poached or hard-boiled egg
Serve with a mixed bean and rice salad and sliced tomatoes.

Sardines, either fresh or canned
Serve on rye toast with chopped dill.

Roast cod with pesto, steamed cauliflower, and green beans
See page 29 for a pesto recipe.

One poached chicken breast
Serve with a mixed salad, roast vegetables, or tabouleh (see p.113).

Sandwich selections

Choose **one** of the following breads:

Gluten-free
Whole grain
Whole wheat
Rye

Top it with your choice of any **one** of the following protein sources:

Cheese—any type, although cottage cheese is the best choice. Try to avoid high-calorie, high-fat blue or aged cheeses.

Egg—use chopped fresh herbs as a flavoring instead of salt, and use minimal quantities of mayonnaise.

Chicken or turkey slices—choose skinless poultry sugar-free deli slices.

Smoked salmon—use minimal quantities of cream cheese with it.

Soups made from vegetables, lentils or beans, and chicken make a **well-balanced** protein and carbohydrate **meal in a bowl**

Choosing to **eat later** on in the evening, perhaps just a **couple of hours** before you go to bed, means that you should **omit** starchy carbohydrates and **increase** the complex carbohydrates from **vegetables** instead

Dinner

In the modern world, dinner has become the main meal of the day. It's the one meal we don't have to rush and is usually eaten in the company of family or friends. This all means we have come to expect more from our evening meal than just eating to keep our energy levels high.

Breakfast and lunch are usually functional meals, but dinner is almost an event by comparison, especially if you eat together as a family or with friends. It is at this time that your good intentions to eat sensibly may falter or be forgotten entirely.

If your last snack was at 4:00PM, aim to eat dinner from 7:00–7:30PM. Try not to eat any later, but if you do, then still eat a small snack at this time, such as a few nuts and an apple or raw vegetables and hummus.

Many dieters will be familiar with the theory that carbohydrates, especially those containing grains, should be limited in the evenings. It isn't necessary to avoid carbohydrates on the Food Doctor plan as long as you eat relatively early. However, if you choose to eat later on in the evening—perhaps just a couple of hours before you go to bed—omit the starchy complex carbohydrates and increase the amount of complex vegetable carbohydrates instead. This means that you include just protein and vegetables at dinner.

If you have an evening meal with family or friends and you can't adhere closely to the Food Doctor plan, go ahead and eat but avoid starchy carbohydrates containing saturated fats. For example, if your meal consists of steak, fries, and salad, omit the fries and eat a large portion of salad and vegetables with your steak instead. This will make your meal healthier than it was even though the steak also contains saturated fat.

Plan ahead

Whatever you prepare, consider making a little extra for the next day. Cooking an extra chicken breast or another portion of fish at the same time will make your next meal or snack that much easier.

THE FOOD DOCTOR DINNER EQUATION

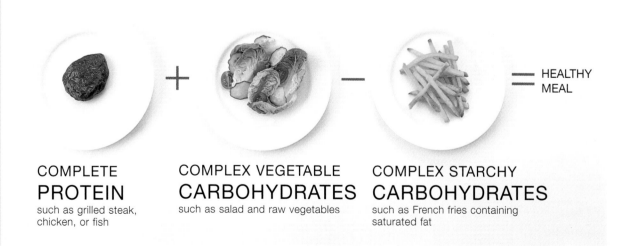

COMPLETE PROTEIN
such as grilled steak, chicken, or fish

COMPLEX VEGETABLE CARBOHYDRATES
such as salad and raw vegetables

COMPLEX STARCHY CARBOHYDRATES
such as French fries containing saturated fat

= HEALTHY MEAL

Dinner suggestions

If you have time in the evenings and you enjoy preparing and cooking food, then be as creative as you can with the meals that you eat. If time is short, however, or if your energy levels are low, then reach for standby ingredients or heat up some homemade soup from the freezer.

There are no prizes for guessing that dinner, just like breakfast and lunch, should combine protein and complex carbohydrates. If you eat your dinner later in the evening, remember to omit the starchy complex carbohydrates, since you won't use the energy they provide.

First, select your protein. Choose from any one of the proteins listed on pages 50–51. These include cod, halibut, chicken, turkey, and eggs.

Then choose your vegetables. It's all too easy to stick to eating the same vegetables all the time, so vary your choices (see pages 52–53).

Rather than seasoning your food with salt, I suggest that you use herbs and spices to enhance the taste of your meal and make it more interesting (see box, below).

Meal suggestions

Thai green chicken curry
Following the recipe on page 126, substitute one chicken breast for the fish and add some chopped cilantro just before serving. Eat with lightly steamed vegetables.

Gingery roast vegetables
Select vegetables such as winter squash or pumpkin, fennel, onions, tomatoes, and zucchini, cut into cubes and put in a shallow dish. Drizzle with olive oil and add a teaspoon of grated ginger. Roast in a medium-hot oven for 45 minutes, then serve with crumbled feta cheese, goat cheese, or slices of mozzarella scattered over the top.

Mixed vegetable soup
Using the tomato and rosemary soup recipe on page 23 as a base, add pieces of raw chicken, fish, or a can

of kidney beans or black-eyed peas when you pour in the stock. If you make fish or bean soup, prepare a larger batch and freeze extra portions to reheat another time.

Grilled Dover sole
Serve with green beans, steamed cauliflower, and hollandaise sauce.

Whole roast trout
Place the cleaned fish in a shallow baking tray, season with freshly ground black pepper, add a bit of butter, and scatter with sliced almonds. Cook in a medium-hot oven for 15 minutes or until the flesh is flaky. Serve with sautéed mushrooms and fennel.

Spicy chicken
Mix a teaspoon each of ground coriander, cumin seeds, crushed garlic and water into a paste. Stuff the inside of a chicken with the spices. Drizzle a little olive oil over, season with freshly ground black pepper, and roast in a medium-hot oven for one hour. Keep half of the chicken aside for a cold meal the next day and serve the rest with grilled vegetables.

Mixed fish stew
See page 124 for a recipe. Serve with lightly steamed vegetables.

Baked mustard mackerel
Mix a tablespoon of sugar-free whole-grain mustard with lemon juice and spread it over the fish. Bake in a medium-hot oven for 10 minutes or so. Serve with a green salad and fresh tomato relish (see p.119).

HERBS AND SPICES

Food can taste very different according to which flavorings you use. Try every herb you can find, either fresh or dried, and select those you like best. Spices can also make a meal more interesting. Try not to overdo fermented sauces such as vinegar and soy sauce (which is highly salted), and instead try low-sodium teriyaki sauce.

General—mint, marjoram, anise, cinnamon, caraway, rosemary, thyme, basil, sage, bay, nutmeg, sorrel, parsley.

Asian—lemongrass, hot chiles, coriander seeds, cilantro, garlic, lemon pepper, ginger, sweet basil.

Indian—curry powder or paste, five-spice paste, garam masala, cumin seeds, cardamom (ground or pods), ginger, garlic.

Quick options

Stir-fried tofu

Add freshly grated ginger, chiles, and red and yellow peppers.

Stir-fried mixed vegetables with chicken or shrimp

Stir-fry the pieces of raw chicken or shrimp first, then add chopped carrots, zucchini, asparagus, baby corn, and herbs of your choice.

Roast asparagus

Place the asparagus in a baking dish, drizzle with olive oil and season with freshly ground black pepper. Cook for 10–15 minutes, then crumble feta cheese over the top and serve.

Chickpea and tomato stew

Use ingredients from your pantry for this recipe. Warm a can each of chickpeas and tomatoes in a small pan over low heat and add chopped fresh basil and parsley. Scatter pumpkin seeds over the top and serve the stew with a selection of grilled vegetables.

Egg salad

Cut two hard-boiled eggs into quarters and serve with cherry tomatoes and a large green salad.

Greek salad

Combine fresh tomatoes, feta cheese, and black olives and serve with a large green salad.

Stir-fried squid

Prepare the squid according to the instructions on page 120. Stir-fry the chopped squid quickly in sunflower oil. Add chopped scallions and bok choy and squeeze over fresh lemon juice just before serving.

Don't worry too much about the occasional feast on **party food**, but try to eat something before you go so that you aren't overly **hungry** when you arrive

Special situations

Life isn't always predictable and, even when you know what your day is likely to hold, there will always be occasions when you will have to adapt the the Food Doctor plan to work for you. Here are a few tips on how to cope with special situations and unexpected food choices.

Eating out

As long as you fully understand the principle of combining proteins with carbohydrates *(see pp. 46–53),* then eating out will be a lot easier than you may think.

The foods to avoid are those that are almost all pure carbohydrates, such as pizza, pasta, risotto, rice, or noodles. For example, in a Chinese restaurant you could choose to order vegetables, fish, and a little steamed rice rather than noodles and fried rice. This selection will help you maintain a beneficial ratio between protein and carbohydrates.

Before you go out, it's always a good idea to eat a small snack, even if it's just a hard-boiled egg, to keep your glucose levels up so that when it is time to eat you aren't so hungry that you make poor food choices.

Finally, be aware that restaurants use significantly more fat in dishes than you would use at home when making a similar dish.

Evening drinks

Going out for a drink right after work can easily result in excessive alcohol intake, followed by a fatty, carbohydrate-loaded take-out meal later in the evening. There is no reason why you shouldn't do this from time to time, but if it's become a regular occurrence, then evenings such as these could be responsible for some of the extra weight that you want to lose.

The best way to minimize the damage is, as always, to eat a snack before you go out. Look at the suggested snacks on pages 82–83 for some ideas, but if you don't have time for a small snack, then eat a few raw, unsalted nuts or olives with your drink and avoid other bar snacks.

Parties

Party foods like crackers and chips are mostly simple carbohydrates, so they will soon leave you feeling hungry for more. But parties are to be enjoyed, so don't worry too much about the occasional party feast. Have a snack, such as a piece of rye bread with cheese, before you go so that you aren't too hungry when you arrive. Eating this sort of snack also helps reduce the speed at which your body absorbs alcohol—because once you have had too much to drink, who cares about losing weight?

On the move

If you are away from home all day and on the move, eat a substantial breakfast and have a package of raw nuts or pumpkin seeds in your bag or briefcase to eat as your midmorning snack. When it comes to lunch, have a sandwich by all means, but buy one with added filling, or discard half of the bread to make one generously filled sandwich so that the ratio of carbohydrates (in this case, bread) to protein (a filling such as meat or fish) is favorable.

Obviously it isn't always going to be easy, so the success of the Food Doctor plan depends on your ability to plan ahead a little and make provisions so that you don't get caught in a situation where you have no choice but to eat the wrong foods. If this does happen—and of course it will sometimes—then just get back on the wagon with the plan when you have your next meal.

Traveling

Whether you travel on a long airplane flight or take a short train ride, you will probably notice that it is harder to find food that fits easily into the Food Doctor plan. So try to plan ahead if you can.

If you are traveling by train, eat something before you leave the house. If the journey is a long one, you will probably need to take some food with you. A container of hummus and crudités makes a convenient snack, while a whole-wheat or rye bread sandwich, generously filled with protein (such as tuna or egg), makes an easy meal.

A plane journey can prove more problematic. Unless you are able to pack a small cooler with snacks like those recommended above, this may be one of those situations when you might not be able to stick to the food plan. If possible, take along a few apples and some raw nuts such as cashews or almonds so that you can at least have a protein and carbohydrate snack as usual. If you are on a short flight, then try to find something healthy to eat at the airport before you fly. If you are on a long flight, then you may find that you are lucky and that the main meal includes a good protein. If not, don't worry about it, go ahead and eat what you are given, and revert to the Plan for Life principles after arrival.

Vacations

Many people try to lose weight before they go on a beach vacation, only to put it all back on again while they are away. I am sure that most of us have heard people say to one another, "Go ahead, you're on vacation," and indulge in foods that won't do anyone any favors. Since the Food Doctor plan is a way of life, you shouldn't find yourself in this predicament. Many of my clients choose to follow the Seven-Day Diet (see pp.14–37) before their vacation to ensure that they feel their best, and then eat sensibly while they are away.

If you are staying in a hotel that includes a continental breakfast as part of the room rate, you may have to invest in an extra breakfast dish to make sure you eat enough protein. Continental breakfasts consist purely of refined carbohydrates, and if you are intending to spend a lazy day on the beach you won't utilize the extra glucose generated by eating this kind of food. Instead, order eggs or cheese and a piece of bread or toast. This choice is far more likely to help you maintain your preferred weight during the vacation.

When it comes to lunch time, limit your alcohol intake and ensure that you include some fish, meat, or poultry in your meal. The same is true for evening meals.

Since it is likely that you will be eating your meals later than you would at home, it is a good idea to have some fruit—preferably hard fruits such as apples—available to keep you going. Keeping a supply of raw nuts is also worthwhile, but don't eat the whole package at once!

You might also want to take some healthy snacks in the car for yourself and any children traveling with you. A couple of plastic containers filled with a few chopped raw vegetables, grapes, cherry tomatoes, and wedges of hard cheese should help them—and you—avoid the last-minute lure of fast-food restaurants and all the unnecessary fats and sugars that their meals contain.

Eating with kids

Many clients tell me that they gain weight because they either pick at their children's food or eat with them at their favorite fast food restaurants. It's all too easy to forget about fueling up yourself while you worry about the kids and then suddenly feel famished as they start to eat. As with all situations, it is best to plan ahead a little. If you pick the children up from school, eat a snack at home first, even if it's just a couple of mouthfuls or leftovers from your last main meal. This will help you resist the fatty, sugary foods that children seem to love. Alternatively, if you want to eat with the children, find something healthy that you can all eat: instead of a burger and fries, choose a lean protein, such as chicken and some vegetables or salad.

How do I cope with eating family meals?

If you have a family, think through your collective favorite foods, the dishes you make or buy that always go over well. Bearing in mind the principles of the Plan for Life, do such meals still fit in? Your family can continue to eat what they want, but you shouldn't forgo all of the foods that you have previously prepared to family acclaim.

Eating dishes different than those of your family at mealtimes can create real problems, so the answer lies in which foods you leave out rather than what you replace them with. For example, if the family meal is pasta with tomato sauce and vegetables, have just a spoonful of pasta and a much larger portion of vegetables. If you cook a roast chicken with all the trimmings, avoid the stuffing and potatoes and enjoy the chicken and vegetables instead. You may have to make some sacrifices, but meals do not have to be dull or unsatisfying.

Take some healthy snacks in the car for yourself and your
children when you travel, to avoid the lure of fast food

Nutrition quiz

Now that you have read through the Plan for Life principles, you will have learned about why I believe it is crucial to eat protein and complex carbohydrates in the right ratios. Now you understand the implications of the correct balance of foods for your well-being, your ability to lose weight, and your desire to be healthy. All that remains is to put the Food Doctor Plan for Life into practice.

Test your knowledge

It's now up to you to apply the Food Doctor plan to your own lifestyle. You will inevitably have to make quick decisions in everyday situations, so if you still feel unfamiliar with any of my principles, look through the book and read them again. The Food Doctor plan is not complicated, but by getting it right you will have a far higher chance of successful weight loss. You can then test your knowledge of the main principles by answering the simple questions in this interactive quiz.

Do you remember the 80:20 rule *(see pp.68–69)*?

How knowledgeable are you?

Now that you have read Plan for Life, put yourself in the following real-life situations to see if you know which are the best options to select.

1 **At a bar, which of the following drinks should you choose?**

☐ A glass of beer?

☐ A glass of red wine?

☐ A vodka and orange juice?

2 **Which is the best choice for a Food Doctor breakfast?**

☐ Sweetened cereal from a box?

☐ Sugar-free muesli containing nuts and a small proportion of dried fruit?

3 At a party, which of the following should you choose?

☐ Cocktail sausages?

☐ Chips?

☐ Nuts?

☐ Pastry shells stuffed with blue cheese?

4 When in a restaurant, which of these meals would be best to choose from the menu?

☐ Minestrone soup as an appetizer, mushroom risotto as a main course, and passion-fruit pavlova for dessert?

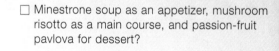

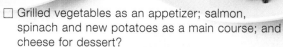

☐ Grilled vegetables as an appetizer; salmon, spinach and new potatoes as a main course; and cheese for dessert?

5 After exercising, which of these snacks should you choose?

☐ Raw nuts?

☐ Granola bar?

☐ Chips?

6 If you can't resist having a coffee, which type should you choose?

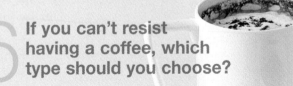

☐ Regular cappuccino?

☐ Latte with skim milk?

☐ Decaffeinated coffee with full-fat milk?

☐ Black filter coffee?

7 At a special occasion which of these should you choose?

☐ Pasta salad?

☐ Potato salad?

☐ Grilled vegetables?

☐ Mozzarella and tomato salad?

8 At dinner time, which of these meals should you choose?

☐ A portion of poached salmon, a small baked potato, and a serving of vegetables?

☐ A large portion of salmon and two large servings of vegetables?

How knowlegeable were you?

1 Red wine
While no alcoholic drink is ideal, red wine is the best choice as long as it is consumed with a meal or snack and not on its own. The vodka is mixed with orange juice—a simple carbohydrate, while the beer contains large quantities of yeast and sugars that encourage bloating.

2 Muesli
The muesli is the best choice as it contains whole grains and nuts, both of which are converted from food to glucose fairly slowly.

3 Raw mixed nuts
Although the nuts are rich in fat, they are the best choice because they contain no saturated fat. Had the pastry shells contained chicken instead of blue cheese, they would have been the preferred choice.

4 Grilled vegetables, salmon, and cheese
The grilled vegetables provide some fiber, while the main course of salmon, potatoes, and vegetables is almost an ideal meal. It supplies the right ratio of protein and complex carbohydrates, unlike the mushroom risotto. The cheese course should always be a small portion rather than a large one.

5

Granola bar

The granola bar will help replenish the glucose that was spent while exercising. Such bars must contain some nuts, and as little sugar and honey as possible.

6

Decaffeinated coffee

While none of the options are ideal (you should not have more than 1–2 cups of coffee a day), the best choice is the decaffeinated coffee. Compared to the caffeinated versions, it is less likely to cause fluctuations in glucose levels, reducing the risk of food cravings.

7

Mozzarella and tomato salad

Mozzarella cheese is a protein, while all the other choices contain carbohydrates. So the combination of cheese and tomato with some olive oil provides the right ratio of protein to complex carbohydrates.

8

Both meals

These meals are both suitable choices as they contain the right ratios of food groups. However, if you were to eat later on in the evening, the meal on the right would be most appropriate, as it omits starchy complex carbohydrates in the form of the baked potato.

Recipes

Some of the recipes in this section are very basic and can be made in just a few minutes, while others need a little more preparation and cooking time. This should give you enough choice to suit your cooking skills and level of interest, and inspire you to try some new and original ideas. Remember that shopping for and cooking with the freshest, healthiest ingredients you can find are crucial to the success of the Food Doctor principles. For those of you who are still reluctant to cook for yourself, try the simplest recipes to begin with. All recipes provide two servings.

Hot apple oatmeal

Oatmeal is a great breakfast standby—delicious and nutritious. Serves two.

4 tablespoons old-fashioned oats
½ cup water
2 tablespoons plain yogurt
1 apple

Place the oats in a small saucepan and pour the water on top. Let the oats soak while you grate the apple, reserving a few slices for a garnish. Add the grated apple to the pan and cook the mixture over low heat until simmering.

Simmer the oatmeal until soft. Divide into two portions, each topped with a tablespoon of yogurt and a few slices of apple.

Yogurt with sweet pear

Choose the ripest, juiciest pears you can find to make this refreshingly tasty meal. Serves two.

1 cup plain yogurt

2 ripe pears, cored and chopped into bite-sized pieces

2 tablespoons sunflower seeds

2 tablespoons pumpkin seeds

Combine the yogurt with the pear and divide into two portions. Sprinkle a tablespoon of each kind of seed over the top of each portion and serve.

Nut-rich muesli

This muesli recipe has plenty of nuts for slow-release energy. To save time in the mornings, you can make a larger quantity and store it in an airtight container where it will keep for up to four weeks. Serves two.

4 tablespoons each of any **4** of the following: barley flakes, rice flakes*, rye flakes, quinoa flakes*, oat flakes, buckwheat flakes*, millet flakes* (*gluten-free)

4 tablespoons mixed nuts, such as hazelnuts, cashew nuts, Brazil nuts, almonds, and walnuts

2 teaspoons each raisins, golden raisins, and dried apple rings (avoid very sweet dried fruit such as mango and pineapple)

Mix all the ingredients together thoroughly and divide into two bowls. Serve with a tablespoon of live natural yogurt and some cows', goats', or sheep's milk or an unsweetened dairy substitute such as rice or soy milk.

Breakfast is the most **important** meal of the day—it boosts your energy to **optimum** levels

Breakfast berries

A **healthy** breakfast will keep you **feeling satisfied** for longer

Set yourself up for the day by relaxing for a moment with a bowl of juicy breakfast berries drizzled with fresh yogurt. Serves two.

Juice and zest 1 orange

50g (2oz) each of any **4** of the following: blackberries, blackcurrants, blueberries, grapes (halved and seeded), raspberries, strawberries

6 each of any **2** of the following: almonds, brazil nuts (chopped), hazelnuts, pistachios

2 tablespoons live natural yogurt

Combine the juice and zest in a bowl, then add the fruit and nuts. Stir thoroughly and divide into two portions. Pour a tablespoon of yogurt over each one and serve with a slice of wholemeal toast.

For an exotic treat, substitute lime juice and zest mixed with a little fresh grated ginger for the orange and tropical fruits such as papaya, pineapple, and mango for the berries.

Baked salmon with fresh herbs

Cooking salmon in foil helps seal in the fresh flavors and keep the fish moist. If you only eat one portion of this hot dish, refrigerate the other serving and eat it cold the next day. Serves two.

8oz (225g) salmon fillets

Juice of ½ lemon

2 scallions, finely sliced

2 tablespoons fresh dill, fennel, and parsley, finely chopped

Preheat the oven to 350°F/180°C.

Brush olive oil lightly over two large squares of aluminum foil. Place a salmon fillet in the middle of each piece of foil, skin side down. Season with freshly ground black pepper, drizzle with lemon juice, and scatter the scallions and herbs on top.

Seal the foil loosely by placing the long edges together and folding over several times. Fold up short ends, place both bundles on a baking tray, and bake for about 15 minutes.

When the fish is just cooked, but still pink inside, divide into two portions and serve (see box, right).

SERVING IDEAS

For lunch Serve with a scoop of brown rice and a salad that includes a few diced raw vegetables and your choice of dressing (see p.117).

For dinner Increase the portion sizes slightly and serve with a large helping of vegetables.

Deviled turkey

This dish has a more intense flavor if you marinate the meat for a few hours in the refrigerator first. The cooked turkey will keep well for up to 24 hours in the refrigerator, but don't reheat it. Serves two.

7oz (200g) turkey breast or cutlets
1 tablespoon mustard
1 tablespoon Worcestershire sauce
Couple of drops Tabasco, more if you prefer

Cut the turkey into large strips. Combine the rest of the ingredients in a shallow dish. Add the turkey and let it marinate for at least 15 minutes, preferably longer.

Remove the turkey from marinade. Cook it under a medium-hot broiler for about 15 minutes, turning occasionally, and serve *(see box, right)*.

> **SERVING IDEAS**
>
> **For lunch** Serve with half of a small baked potato per person and a mixed salad.
>
> **For dinner** Increase the portion sizes slightly and serve with three different steamed vegetables.

Asian stir-fry

Stir-frying is a healthy option, since only a small amount of oil is used. If you can't find these exotic ingredients easily, substitute other greens and brown or button mushrooms. Serves two.

SERVING IDEAS

For lunch Serve with a few rice noodles and steamed bean sprouts.

For dinner Add more fibrous vegetables to the stir-fry and omit the rice noodles.

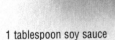

1 tablespoon soy sauce

1 teaspoon Thai fish sauce

1 teaspoon five-spice powder

1 teaspoon tomato paste

1 small clove garlic, crushed

2 heads bok choy, stalks and leaves shredded

4–6 large brown mushrooms, sliced

4–6 mixed exotic mushrooms, left whole or sliced the same size as the brown mushrooms, depending on the variety and size

1 tablespoon pumpkin seeds

1 teaspoon sesame seeds

Mix the soy sauce, fish sauce, five-spice paste, and tomato paste together and set aside.

Heat the wok over low heat. Then add a tablespoon of olive oil and soften the garlic. Turn up the heat and add the bok choy. Stir-fry for one minute until the leaves wilt.

Stir in the mushrooms until they are coated with oil and beginning to soften. Add the sauce mixture and the pumpkin and sesame seeds. Stir well and serve immediately.

• To add protein to this recipe, use 4oz (100g) of chicken, turkey, or fish cut into strips, and stir-fry the strips first, before adding the bok choy.

• For a vegetarian option, cut 4oz (100g) of tofu into cubes and add at the same time as the mushrooms.

Tabouleh

This recipe requires up to an hour of standing time, so allow plenty of time. It keeps for up to three days in the refrigerator. Serves two.

½ cup couscous or bulgur wheat

2 cups water

½ small cucumber, diced

2 medium tomatoes, diced and seeded

Juice of 1 lemon

Small bunch each of fresh mint and parsley, finely chopped

1 tablespoon olive oil

Soak the couscous in the water for 30 minutes, then drain, squeezing out any excess moisture. Mix in the cucumber, tomatoes, and lemon juice, and season with black pepper.

Set aside for 30 minutes more. Then add the herbs and olive oil, toss well, and serve *(see box, right)*.

SERVING IDEAS

For lunch Add a spoonful of tabouleh to your protein, along with a mixed salad.

For dinner Have a small spoonful as part of your main meal if you eat before 7:00PM. If you eat later, omit this dish.

Tamarind chicken

Tamarind, the sticky pulp of the beanlike fruit from a tropical evergreen tree, has a sour taste with a hint of sweetness. If possible, marinate the chicken for a couple of hours before you cook it. Leftovers can be stored in the refrigerator and eaten cold the next day. Serves two.

2 teaspoons tamarind paste
1 large clove garlic, crushed
1 teaspoon lemon juice
8oz (225g) chicken breast cutlets
Few sprigs fresh parsley, chopped

SERVING IDEAS

For lunch Serve with a couple of new potatoes and steamed vegetables drizzled with a little olive oil.

For dinner Increase the portion sizes slightly and serve with a salad or steamed vegetables.

Combine the tamarind paste, garlic, and lemon juice in a shallow bowl. Add the chicken and coat in the mixture. Marinate for at least 15 minutes, and ideally for an hour or two.

Remove the chicken from the marinade and place under a medium broiler for about 15 minutes, turning occasionally. Slice cooked chicken into thin strips, scatter the parsley on top, and serve hot or cold *(see box, above right)*.

Fish fillet with lime

Buy good-quality fish for this dish; it will be fresher and more flavorful. Buy the smallest package of chickpea flour you can find and use it quickly; it tends to lose its freshness after a short while. Serves two.

SERVING IDEAS
For lunch Serve with vegetables and a small scoop of mashed potatoes.
For dinner Increase the portion sizes slightly and serve with vegetables.

7oz (200g) firm white fish fillets

Juice of ½ lime

1 large clove garlic, sliced

½ cup chickpea flour (available in Indian markets) or cornmeal

Few sprigs fresh parsley, chopped

½ lime, cut into wedges

3 tablespoons vegetable oil

Cut the fish into wide strips. Place in a shallow dish, squeeze the lime juice over the top, and season with freshly ground black pepper.

Heat the oil in a frying pan and warm over low heat. Cook the garlic for about five minutes, then discard.

In a separate shallow dish, sprinkle the flour in a thin layer. Lift the fish from the juice, coat it in the flour, and cook in the garlic-flavored oil for one minute on each side until golden. Lift out the pieces with a slotted spoon, drain on paper towels for a few seconds, and divide between two plates. Scatter with parsley and lime wedges and serve (*see box, above right*).

Salade niçoise

This variation on a traditional salade niçoise—which contains canned tuna and hard-boiled eggs—can be adapted to include your preferred choice of protein. Serves two.

SERVING IDEAS

For lunch Add 2oz (50g) tuna or a hard-boiled egg and a piece of rye toast per serving.

For dinner Omit toast; increase tuna portion, or divide three eggs between two servings.

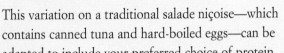

Handful of green beans, cut into short lengths

Handful of sugar snap peas or snow peas

Handful of chicory, red-leaf lettuce, or Boston lettuce

6 cherry tomatoes, halved

½ yellow pepper, finely sliced

2-4 brown mushrooms, sliced

6–8 pitted black olives

2 tablespoons cooked or canned red kidney beans

Few herbs such as basil, arugula, or fresh fennel, chopped

Steam the beans and peas together for about 10 minutes until they are just cooked but still slightly crunchy.

Let the vegetables cool while you tear the lettuce leaves and arrange them in a salad bowl. Layer the salad with the remaining ingredients, scattering the fresh herbs over the top.

Use a simple French dressing (*see opposite page*) and toss the ingredients well just before serving (*see box, above*).

Salad dressings

Simple French dressing

2 tablespoons olive oil

1 teaspoon cider vinegar

½ teaspoon Dijon mustard

Combine the ingredients well using a small hand whisk and season with freshly ground black pepper. The dressing will keep in the refrigerator for up to one week.

Asian dressing

3 tablespoons olive oil

1 tablespoon soy sauce

1 tablespoon lime juice

½ teaspoon five-spice powder

Mix the ingredients well using a small hand whisk. This dressing can be kept in the freezer for up to one month.

Vegetable juice dressing

½ cup organic vegetable juice

¼ cup lemon juice

¼ cup olive oil

Blend the ingredients well using a small hand whisk and season with freshly ground black pepper. For more punch, add one crushed clove of garlic. This dressing freezes well for up to one month.

Avocado dressing

1 ripe avocado

1 cup plain yogurt

Peel and pit the avocado. To retain some texture in the dressing, use a fork to mash the avocado roughly with the yogurt. Season with freshly ground black pepper and keep the dressing in the refrigerator for up to 24 hours.

Simple chickpea purée

With its creamy taste and nutty aroma, this purée forms a nutritious and versatile basis for a quick meal. It may be refrigerated for up to three days. Serves two.

15oz (425g) canned chickpeas, drained and rinsed

2 sprigs fresh thyme or ½ teaspoon dried thyme

1 large clove garlic

3 tablespoons plain yogurt

Put the chickpeas, thyme and garlic into a small pan and cover with water. Bring to boil and simmer gently for 15 minutes.

Drain the chickpeas and put them in a bowl. Remove the fresh thyme. Add the yogurt and mash by hand for a coarse purée, or mix in a blender for a smoother texture.

Vegetables stuffed with chickpea purée

2 tablespoons chickpea purée

Few sprigs fresh parsley, chopped

Lemon juice and a little lemon zest for added flavor

2 medium tomatoes with the tops cut off and pulp removed, or 1 large red or yellow pepper, halved and de-seeded

Olive oil

Preheat the oven to 350°F/180°C.

Mix the purée, parsley, lemon juice and zest. Fill the pepper or tomatoes with purée, place in a baking dish, season with black pepper, and drizzle with olive oil. Cover with foil and bake for 30 minutes. Serve with a mixed green salad.

Avocado stuffed with chickpea purée

2 tablespoons chickpea purée

Lemon juice and a little lemon zest

1 ripe avocado

1 tomato, chopped

Mix the chickpea purée with the lemon juice and zest and season with freshly ground black pepper to taste.

Cut the avocado in half, remove the pit, and fill with the purée. Serve each half on a plate with the chopped tomato scattered across the top.

Falafel

These spicy Moroccan chickpea burgers can be eaten hot or cold. They keep in the freezer for up to a month. Serves two.

15oz (425g) canned chickpeas, drained and rinsed

1 large clove garlic

1 small onion, chopped

1 teaspoon ground coriander

1 teaspoon ground cumin

1 heaping tablespoon buckwheat flour

2 medium tomatoes, roughly chopped and mixed with the juice of 1 lemon and a drizzle of olive oil

1 cup plain yogurt mixed with ½ teaspoon each of cayenne pepper and turmeric powder

Blend the chickpeas, garlic, onion, and spices in a food processor until almost smooth. Scrape the paste into a bowl and mix in the flour. Divide into eight balls, each about the size of a golf ball. Flatten into patties.

Coat the bottom of a frying pan with olive oil and gently brown the falafels on each side—they should all fit in at once. Add a little more oil, if needed, when you turn them.

Serve the falafel with the tomato relish and yogurt mix.

Squid in a fresh tomato sauce

Squid is easy to prepare, but you can ask a fishmonger to cut and clean it for you, or buy it precleaned. If you want to make extra portions, this dish can be frozen for up to one month and then reheated gently. Serves two.

1lb (450g) squid
1 medium onion, chopped
1 large clove garlic, crushed
3 medium tomatoes, peeled and diced
1 tablespoon lemon juice and a little zest
¼ teaspoon saffron threads, crushed in a spoon with a little water
Handful of fresh parsley and cilantro, chopped

To prepare the squid, pull the head from the sac to draw out the innards and spine. Scrape off the pinkish outside membrane from the sac, rinse the sac, and cut into rings. Sever the tentacles from the head, cut into pieces, and rinse.

Soften the onion in a little olive oil in a small pan, then add the garlic and stir for two minutes. Add the tomatoes, lemon juice, zest, and saffron. Stir in the squid and pour in just enough water to cover. Simmer for five minutes until the squid is opaque but not rubbery.

Stir in the herbs and serve with a scoop of brown rice and a green salad with an olive oil and lemon dressing.

Tabouleh South American style

Keep this tasty salad in an airtight container in the
refrigerator for up to three days and serve a spoonful
of it with a portion of chicken and fish. Serves two.

½ cup quinoa

1 cup water, with a pinch of bouillon powder added

½ seedless cucumber, diced

2 medium tomatoes, diced

2 scallions, finely sliced

Juice of ½ lemon

Small bunch each of fresh mint and parsley, finely chopped

1 tablespoon olive oil

Gently simmer the quinoa and water in a small pan for
15 minutes or so until all the water is absorbed.

Meanwhile, chop the remaining ingredients. Once the
quinoa has cooled, stir in the vegetables. Transfer to a bowl
and put the mixture into the refrigerator for 10–15
minutes to allow the flavors to develop. Season with
freshly ground black pepper and serve.

Always serve a **small portion** of starchy carbohydrates with protein and vegetables at lunchtime

Pipérade

A wonderfully simple dish to prepare and cook, pipérade makes a perfect instant supper and should be eaten immediately, while piping hot. Serves two.

1 small onion, sliced

1 yellow pepper, seeded and cut into strips

2 medium tomatoes, peeled and sliced

Pinch cayenne pepper

1 sprig fresh mint, chopped

2 large eggs

In a frying pan coated with olive oil, soften the onion and pepper over low heat until the onions are golden. Add the tomatoes, cayenne pepper, and mint, and stir briefly.

Either break the eggs on top of the vegetables or beat them first and add to the pan so they cook like scrambled eggs. Cook gently until the eggs set, then serve.

Watercress and carrot soup

This recipe is worth freezing if you want to save one serving or make up a larger batch of individual portions to defrost for an instant meal another day. Serves two.

1 small onion, chopped

3 large carrots, chopped

1 bunch fresh watercress

8oz (225g) canned chickpeas

3 cups vegetable, mushroom, or chicken stock; fresh is best but canned broth or bouillon cubes are also fine

1 teaspoon ground cumin

Gently heat a tablespoon of olive oil in a medium-sized saucepan; add onion and soften. Add the chopped carrots and soften for five minutes.

Chop the watercress straight into the pan, stalks and all, using scissors. Stir well until the watercress is mixed in and begins to wilt. Add the chickpeas, stock, and cumin and simmer gently for 20 minutes or so, until the carrots are just cooked. Blend the soup in a processor until smooth, season with freshly ground black pepper, and serve.

The Food Doctor soups are full of **nutrients** and can easily be augmented with extra protein for a **delicious** meal.

Easy fish chowder

This stewlike soup is full of nutrients. Don't use dried bouillon cubes for this recipe; buy ready-made fresh stock from a good fish market, or make your own. Freeze any extra portions, then defrost and gently reheat them. Serves two.

4oz (100g) white fish fillet, cut into bite-sized chunks

Juice of ½ lemon

1 medium onion, chopped

2 large cloves garlic, crushed

2 cups fish stock

3 medium tomatoes, peeled and chopped

1 bay leaf

4oz (100g) cooked mixed seafood

3oz (75g) canned or white beans, drained

Few sprigs each cilantro, parsley, and dill, chopped

Marinate the fish in the lemon juice while you prepare the rest of the ingredients.

Soften the onion and garlic in a tablespoon of olive oil over low heat in a medium-sized saucepan. Add the stock, tomatoes, bay leaf, and white fish. Simmer very gently for about five minutes.

Add the seafood and beans and simmer two minutes more until the seafood has heated through thoroughly. Season with freshly ground black pepper, stir in the herbs, and serve.

Garlic broccoli with feta cheese

If you find feta cheese too salty, rinse the block of cheese under cold running water before you cube it. This dish can be eaten hot or cold. Serves two.

4oz (100g) feta cheese, cut into small cubes

2 teaspoons lemon juice

2 teaspoons olive oil

Several sprigs fresh parsley, chopped

Freshly ground black pepper to taste

1 clove garlic, crushed or finely chopped

½ bunch broccoli, cut into small florets

4 sun-dried tomatoes, cut into thin strips

Marinate the feta cheese in the lemon juice, olive oil, chopped parsley, and freshly ground black pepper while you cook the broccoli.

Coat the bottom of a frying pan with additional olive oil, add the garlic, and cook for one minute. Then add the broccoli and sun-dried tomatoes, stirring occasionally until the broccoli is tender but still firm to the bite.

Lift the feta cheese out of the marinade with a slotted spoon and add to the frying pan. Gently stir the ingredients and serve with the remaining marinade poured on top.

Monkfish curry with carrot salad

The monkfish in this recipe can easily be replaced with other firm white fish such as cod or haddock, or even strips of chicken breast if you prefer. Serves two.

Salad

2 large carrots, grated

1 heaping teaspoon black mustard seeds

1 teaspoon lemon juice

Heat a tablespoon of olive oil in a small pan. Once hot, add the mustard seeds. As the seeds begin to pop (it only takes a few seconds), lift the pan from the heat and pour the oil and seeds over the raw carrots. Add the lemon juice and toss.

Let cool while you cook the monkfish.

Curry

1 tablespoon green curry paste

9oz (250g) monkfish, cut into bite-sized chunks

2–3 kaffir lime leaves, torn

1 stalk lemongrass, bruised and chopped

½ cup canned coconut milk

1 tablespoon Thai fish sauce

½ seedless cucumber, cut into batons

12 basil leaves, torn roughly by hand

Heat a tablespoon of olive oil in a medium-sized pan over low heat, add the curry paste, and cook for a minute. Add the monkfish, lime leaves, and lemongrass. Cook gently for two minutes, stirring occasionally.

Stir in the coconut milk and simmer for five minutes or until fish is tender. Stir in the fish sauce, cucumber, and the basil leaves, and serve with the carrot salad.

Hot and sour chicken salad

You need to plan a couple of hours ahead with this recipe to allow enough time to let the chicken marinate and the flavors develop. Serves two.

1 large chicken breast fillet, skinned and sliced thinly

For the marinade:

½ in (1cm) fresh ginger root, peeled and grated

1 small clove garlic, chopped

2 teaspoons crunchy peanut butter

1 tablespoon fresh coriander, chopped, plus extra to garnish

1 tablespoon cider vinegar

1 teaspoon Thai fish sauce

1 tablespoon olive oil

Salad

1 cup bean sprouts

¼ head napa cabbage, shredded

1 medium carrot, cut into sticks

1 small red onion, finely sliced into rings

1 teaspoon sesame seeds

1 tablespoon cilantro, chopped

Combine the marinade ingredients in a small bowl, add the chicken pieces, and marinate for a couple of hours in the refrigerator.

Heat the olive oil in a wok over a high heat, remove the chicken from the marinade and stir-fry it for about five minutes, until the meat is cooked through but not browned.

Mix together the salad ingredients and arrange on two plates. Transfer the chicken to the plates, scatter with sesame seeds and cilantro and serve immediately.

Leek and quinoa risotto

DINNER

Serve this dish with a crisp mixed salad, tossed in your choice of dressing (*see p.117*), to set off the soft texture of the leeks and quinoa. Any extra portions can be frozen for up to one month. Serves two.

2 small leeks

1 cup water, with a pinch of bouillon powder added

¼ cup olive oil

1 tablespoon tomato paste

½ cup quinoa

1 large portobello mushroom, thickly sliced

2 teaspoons ground coriander

1 tablespoon fresh parsley, chopped

Juice of ½ lemon

Slice the white parts of the leeks only into ½ in (1cm) rings and rinse well. Pour the water and oil into a medium-sized saucepan, add the leeks and tomato paste, and bring to a boil. Simmer for five minutes, then add the quinoa, mushrooms, and coriander.

Simmer for 15 minutes more until the water is absorbed. Stir in the parsley and lemon juice, season with black pepper, and serve with a salad.

Lentils with fresh ginger

To make cardamom seeds into a powder, simply split several cardomom pods with a small, sharp knife, put the seeds into a mortar, and grind them using a pestle. Use packaged cardamon powder if you prefer. Serves two.

1¼ cups dried lentils

1 cup vegetable stock

1 small onion, chopped

1 clove garlic, crushed

¾ in (2cm) fresh ginger root, grated

1 teaspoon cardamom seeds, ground, or cardamom powder

3 large ripe tomatoes, peeled and chopped

1 tablespoon sunflower seeds

2 tablespoons cilantro, chopped

Bring the lentils and stock to a boil in a medium-sized pan, cover, and simmer over low heat for 30 minutes, until the lentils are soft but not mushy. Drain the lentils and set aside.

In the same pan, soften the onion and garlic in olive oil over low heat. Stir in the ginger, cardamom, and almost all the tomatoes, reserving some for a garnish. Cook for a few minutes.

Return the lentils to the pan and season with freshly ground black pepper. Heat thoroughly. Then arrange lentils on two plates, top with sunflower seeds and cilantro, and serve with a green salad.

Freeze fresh meals such as this to **build** a stock of nutritious instant **meals**

Fish with roasted vegetables

Any firm, white fish steak or fillet is suitable for this recipe. Avoid overcooking the fish so that it does not become too dry. Serves two.

1lb (450g) white fish steak or fillet, such as haddock or cod, skinned

Squeeze of lemon juice

1 medium zucchini, cut into chunks

1 medium onion, sliced

1 clove garlic, chopped

3 medium tomatoes, halved

1 sprig fresh rosemary

2 tablespoons olive oil

2 teaspoons cider vinegar

Preheat oven to 400°F/200°C.

Season the fish with freshly ground black pepper and lemon juice, then cover the fish and set aside.

Put the vegetables and herbs in an ovenproof dish and toss them in the olive oil, vinegar, and some black pepper. Roast uncovered for 30 minutes, stirring every ten minutes.

Brush the fish with olive oil and set it on top of the vegetables. Cook in the oven for 5–10 minutes more until the fish is just cooked. Serve immediately with a green salad.

Mediterranean braised chicken

DINNER

This recipe relies on good-quality ingredients for its delicious flavor, so use the best olives available and pick ripe, juicy tomatoes. You may want to have the thighs for dinner and save the legs to eat cold the next day. Serves two.

2 dark-meat chicken quarters (thigh and leg)

1 small onion, finely sliced

3 ripe medium tomatoes, sliced, or 14oz (400g) canned tomatoes

1 teaspoon mixed Herbes de Provence

Juice of ½ lemon

1 cup stock, either chicken or vegetable

8 large black olives

½ cup cooked or canned red kidney beans

Skin the chicken quarters and cut each at the joint In a shallow casserole dish or frying pan with a lid, lightly brown the chicken pieces in olive oil over high heat. Remove the browned chicken from the pan and put to one side.

Add a little more oil if necessary and gently soften the onion and tomatoes, together with the herbs and lemon juice, for five minutes. Add the olives and beans and ½ cup of the stock, then season with black pepper to taste.

Add the chicken, cover, and cook over very low heat for about 45 minutes until the chicken is cooked through and tender. Add stock during cooking if necessary. The slow cooking will give the chicken a rich flavor. Serve with a green salad.

Asian chicken

Allow at least half an hour between preparing the
ingredients and cooking the chicken so that it can
fully absorb the flavors of the marinade. Serves two.

1 small bunch cilantro, roughly chopped

2 garlic cloves, roughly chopped

2 hot chiles, with or without seeds, roughly chopped

1in (2½cm) fresh ginger, grated

Juice and zest of 1 lime

4 tablespoons light soy sauce

2 chicken breasts, skinned and lightly scored

Place all the ingredients except the chicken breasts in
a bowl, season with black pepper, and mix well. Lay each
chicken breast on a large piece of foil and rub the mixture
over the chicken. Seal the foil, making two bundles, and
set aside to marinate for at least 30 minutes.

Preheat the oven to 400°F/200°C.

Bake the chicken in the foil for 30 minutes, or until the
meat is cooked. Transfer the chicken to two plates and
serve with a green salad.

Lime chicken with a bean salad

This chicken recipe is worth cooking and freezing as individual portions if you want some instant suppers from the freezer over the next three weeks or so. Serves two.

2 skinned chicken breasts, about 4oz (100g) for each portion
Juice and zest of 2 fresh limes
2 cloves garlic, finely chopped
Handful of oyster mushrooms, roughly chopped
Handful of cilantro, roughly chopped

Cut the chicken breasts into strips about ½in (1cm) thick. Combine in a shallow bowl with the lime juice and zest, chopped garlic, and a seasoning of freshly ground pepper. Set aside for about 15 minutes to allow the chicken to absorb the flavors.

Heat two tablespoons of olive oil in a wok or frying pan over high heat. Remove the chicken from the marinade and sear in the hot oil. Reduce heat, add the marinade, and cook for five minutes. Add the mushrooms and cilantro, cook for another minute or so, and serve with the bean salad.

Salad

4oz (100g) thin green beans, trimmed
4oz (100g) snow peas, shredded diagonally
4oz (100g) bean sprouts (about 1 cup)
½ small red onion, finely sliced in rings
Handful of cilantro, chopped

Steam the green beans and snow peas for three minutes. Drain and run under cold water to refresh the vegetables. In a large bowl, mix the blanched vegetables with the other ingredients and splash with Asian salad dressing *(see p.117)*.

Classic guacamole

Use this creamy dip as a snack with crudités such as carrots, scallions, cherry tomatoes, raw broccoli, and cauliflower. Serves two.

2 ripe avocados
2 teaspoons grated onion
1 tablespoon mixed pumpkin, sunflower, and sesame seeds
1 small clove garlic, crushed
2 teaspoons lemon juice
2 teaspoons olive oil
Pinch of cayenne pepper
Dash of Worcestershire sauce
Dash of Tabasco

Mash the avocados with the onion, seeds, garlic, lemon juice, and olive oil in a small bowl. Add black pepper, cayenne pepper, Worcestershire sauce, and Tabasco to taste.

Cover tightly with plastic wrap, and let the flavors develop for half an hour in the refrigerator before serving.

Fruit smoothie

Adapt this recipe to include your favorite seasonal fruits such as blackberries, peaches, apricots, and plums. Extra portions keep in the refrigerator for up to 24 hours. Serves two.

2 cups plain yogurt
1 apple, peeled and cored
1 large ripe pear, peeled and cored
2 tablespoons pumpkin seeds, unsalted
Pinch of cinnamon

Put the yogurt, apple, pear, and pumpkin seeds into a food processor and blend until smooth. Pour into large cups, top with cinnamon, and serve.

Have a delicious **protein-rich** smoothie as a **refreshing** midmorning or midafternoon **snack**.

Hard-boiled eggs with crudités

Keep these eggs and crudités in an airtight container in the refrigerator for up to two days to have as an instant snack. If you are a vegan, substitute small chunks of tofu for the eggs. Serves two.

6 quail eggs or 2 hen's eggs

8 black olives

Approximately 9oz (250g) of a selection of raw vegetables—for example, carrots, broccoli, cauliflower, peppers, cherry tomatoes, cucumber, or celery—in small, almost bite-sized pieces

Hard-boil the eggs and let cool. Either leave the eggs whole in their shells, or remove the shell and cut the eggs into quarters. Arrange the eggs on a plate with the olives and raw vegetables to serve.

Vegetable frittata

Eat one serving of this frittata while hot, then refrigerate the other portion for up to two days to be eaten cold. Serves two.

1 medium onion, chopped

9oz (250g) spinach after removing any thick stems, rinsed and roughly torn

Freshly ground pepper

Pinch of nutmeg

2 medium tomatoes, peeled and chopped

4oz (100g) canned chickpeas or white beans

4 large eggs

Drizzle of olive oil

In a large saucepan, soften the onion in olive oil over low heat Add the spinach, pepper, nutmeg, and tomatoes, and cook until most of the liquid has evaporated. Then add the chickpeas or beans.

Lightly whisk the eggs and season with pepper. Place a large frying pan over low heat and coat with olive oil. When the oil is hot, pour in half of the egg mixture, immediately followed by the vegetables and the rest of the eggs. Stir gently, cover with a lid and cook over low heat for 10 minutes or so until set.

Brown under the broiler. Cut wedges to serve.

Glossary

Adrenaline
A hormone secreted by the adrenal glands (located above the kidneys) in response to low blood-glucose levels, exercise, or stress. Adrenaline causes an increase in blood-sugar levels by breaking down glycogen stores to glucose in the liver, encouraging the release of fatty acids from body tissue, causing blood vessels to dilate and increasing cardiac output.

Amino acids
Amino acids form the basic constituents of proteins. There are nine essential amino acids that cannot be produced by the body and must be supplied by food, although the ninth is only considered essential for children.

Bacteria
Micro-organisms found in soil, air, water, and food. Some bacteria are harmful and cause disease, others are beneficial, including many of those that live in the intestine and which help to break down food for digestion.

Blood-glucose levels
The concentration of glucose in the blood.

Cardiovascular
Relating to the heart and blood vessels.

Chyme
The pulpy, acidic, semi-liquid product of partly digested food that passes from the stomach to the small intestine.

Complex carbohydrate
A food containing insoluble fiber, which helps to slow down the process of digestion.

Diuretic effect
Increases the rate of urination, generally decreasing water retention.

Enzyme
A protein molecule that acts as a catalyst in bringing about biological reactions in the body. Enzymes are essential for normal function.

Essential fats
Fats that are essential to the normal functioning of the body, but which cannot be created by the body and so have to be derived from foods. Omega-3 essential fats are found in oily fish, such as mackerel, salmon, herring, tuna, and sardines, and also in flax and hemp seeds. Omega-6 oils are found in most seeds and nuts except peanuts.

Fiber
Mostly derived from plant cell walls, fiber is not broken down by digestive enzymes but may be partly digested by beneficial bacteria in the gut. Fiber is essential for good digestive health: insoluble fiber provides bulk to the feces and so helps to prevent constipation; soluble fiber helps to reduce blood-cholesterol levels and eliminate toxins and excess hormones.

Free radical
A naturally occurring, short-lived, highly unstable molecule that is usually produced when chemical reactions occur in the body. In its search for stability it will "steal" an electron from another molecule, causing it to become a free radical. This results in a cascade of free radical activity, which can result in the deterioration of tissue and degeneration associated with aging, cancer, Alzheimer's, Parkinson's disease, and arthritis, among many. Stress, pollution, poor diet, excessive sun exposure, smoking, radiation, and illness all increase the build-up of free radicals.

Gliadin
A protein that constitutes gluten. Intolerance to gliadin is known as coeliac disease.

Glucose
A simple form of sugar, also known as a monosaccharide. It occurs naturally in various foods—for example, in some fruits—and is the body's main source of fuel. Carbohydrates are broken down into glucose by the body. However, body cells cannot use glucose without the help of insulin.

Gluten
An insoluble protein group that is found in wheat, rye, barley, and oats. Gluten is the mixture of proteins, which includes gliadin, to which celiacs are intolerant.

Glycemic index
The glycemic index ranks foods on a scale of 1–100 on how they affect blood-glucose levels. This index measures how much blood sugar increases in the two or three hours after eating. Foods that are broken down quickly during the process of digestion have the highest GI values (70 and above)—they make blood-glucose levels rise high quickly. Foods that are broken down slowly, releasing glucose gradually into the bloodstream, have low GI scores (under 55).

Hydrochloric acid
Hydrochloric acid, or stomach acid, is the acid component of gastric juice. It plays a number of important roles in the process of digestion, including creating the right acidic environment for protein digestion to occur and killing many pathogens present in food.

Insulin
The hormone insulin is produced by the pancreas and helps glucose to enter the body's cells where it is used up as fuel. Insulin is also a storage hormone in that it will cause any excess glucose that is not needed immediately for energy to be stored as glycogen in the liver or muscles, or converted to fat and stored in body tissue.

Irritable bowel syndrome (IBS)
Irritable bowel syndrome, also known as spastic colon, is a common disorder whereby the regular waves of muscular movement along the intestines become uncoordinated. This disruption, involving both the small intestine and the colon, results in a variety of symptoms in all areas of the digestive tract, including intermittent diarrhea and constipation, cramp-like abdominal pain, and swelling of the abdomen.

Metabolic rate
The energy required to keep the body functioning while at rest.

Metabolism
The "burning" of glucose in body cells to produce energy.

Minerals

Substances, such as calcium, magnesium, and iron, that are naturally found in various foods and which are required by the body for the maintenance of good health. A balanced, healthy diet usually contains all the minerals the body requires.

Mitochondria

Found in the cytoplasm of every cell in the body. Due to their role in the production of energy-molecules, known as ATP, mitochondria are considered the "powerhouses" of cells.

Nutrients

Vital substances required by all living organisms for survival.

Organic produce

Food that has been produced using farming methods that severely restrict the use of artificial chemical fertilizers and pesticides, and animals reared without the routine use of drugs, antibiotics, and wormers common in intensive livestock farming.

Osteoporosis

A condition in which the density of bones declines, making them brittle and prone to fracture. The mineral calcium is essential for bone health.

Pathogen

Any micro-organism that causes disease, for example, a parasite.

Parasite

An organism that lives off and obtains food from another organism or host. Giardia is an example of a parasite that may be found in the gut.

Protein

A complex compound, made of carbon, hydrogen, oxygen, and nitrogen and often sulphur, which is essential to all living things. Protein is required for growth and repair and is broken down into amino acids by the body.

Saliva

An alkaline liquid secreted by the salivary glands into the mouth. Saliva lubricates food, helping in the process of chewing and swallowing, and contains an enzyme that helps to break down the starch in foods. It also has antibacterial properties.

Simple carbohydrate

A food that yields simple sugars, which are broken down rapidly into glucose by the body.

Saturated fats

Saturated fats are primarily animal fats that are solid at room temperature. Such fats are found in meat and dairy produce. Coconut oil is the only vegetable oil that contains a significant amount of saturated fats. Saturated fats have been shown to raise the levels of "bad" LDL (low-density lipoprotein) cholesterol in the blood.

Stimulants

Substances, including caffeine, found in foods and drinks, such as chocolate and fizzy drinks, that stimulate the production of adrenaline from the adrenal glands. Under normal circumstances, this release of adrenaline prepares the body for the "flight or fight" response syndrome, causing—among many things—the heart to beat faster. If adrenaline is overproduced because stimulant foods have been consumed, this may lead to fatigue and blood-glucose imbalances in the body.

Type 2 diabetes

Diabetes mellitus is a condition in which blood-glucose levels can become dangerously high because the body cannot utilize glucose properly. Excess blood-glucose levels (hyperglycemia) can result in long-term damage to the eyes, kidneys, nerves, heart, and major arteries. There are two principal types of diabetes: insulin-dependent Type 1 diabetes, and non-insulin dependent Type 2 diabetes, also known as adult-onset diabetes. In Type 2 diabetes the body cannot make enough insulin, or cell receptors do not respond to insulin (also known as insulin resistance). This type of diabetes usually

occurs in people over the age of 40, although it is becoming increasingly common in the younger population due to an increase in high-sugar, refined carbohydrate diets— even teenagers are now being diagnosed.

Villi

Fine, fingerlike protrusions that cover the lining of the small intestines and which help to increase the surface area, thereby increasing the ability of the intestine to absorb nutrients.

Vitamins

Groups of complex organic substances, found in many different foods, that are essential in small amounts for the normal functioning of the body. There are 13 vitamins. With the exception of vitamin D and niacin, which can be generated by the body, vitamins must be obtained from your diet. A varied diet will contain adequate amounts of all the vitamins.

Yeast

A single cell organism used in some food industry processes such as baking, brewing, and winemaking. Some yeasts become pathogens once inside the body (for example, *Candida albicans*, which causes thrush) and may cause infection in any open canal in the body such as the vagina, ear, or mouth. Excess sugar, alcohol, stress, and antibiotics can cause a proliferation in pathogenic yeasts.

Useful addresses and websites

Please note that, due to the fast-changing nature of the worldwide web, some websites may be out of date by the time you read this.

ORGANIZATIONS IN THE US

The American College of Cardiology
Heart House
9111 Old Georgetown Road
Bethesda, MD 20814-1699
tel: (800) 253-4636
www.acc.org

American College of Gastroenterology
P.O. Box 3099
Alexandria, VA 22302
tel: (703) 820-7400
www.acg.gi.org

American Diabetes Association
1701 North Beauregard Street
Alexandria, VA 22311
tel: (800) DIABETES
www.diabetes.org

American Dietetic Association
120 South Riverside Plaza
Suite 2000
Chicago, IL 60606-6995
tel: (800) 877-1600
www.eatright.org

American Gastroenterological Association
4930 Del Ray Avenue,
Bethesda, MD 20814
tel: (301) 654-2055
www.gastro.org

American Heart Association National Center
7272 Greenville Avenue
Dallas, TX 75231
tel: (800) AHA-USA-1
www.americanheart.org

Asthma and Allergy Foundation of America
1233 20th Street, NW
Suite 402
Washington, DC 20036
tel: (800) 7-ASTHMA
www.aafa.org

Celiac Disease Foundation
13251 Ventura Blvd. #1
Studio City, CA 91604
tel: (818) 990-2354
www.celiac.org

Celiac Sprue Association
PO Box 31700
Omaha, NE 68131-0700
tel: (402) 558-0600
www.csaceliacs.org

Crohn's & Colitis Foundation of America
386 Park Avenue South, 17th Floor
New York, NY 10016
tel: (800) 932-2423
www.ccfa.org

Food and Nutrition Information Center
National Agricultural Library, Room 105
10301 Baltimore Avenue
Beltsville, MD 20705-2351
tel: 301-504-5719
www.nal.usda.gov/fnic

Irritable Bowel Syndrome Association
1440 Whalley Ave. #145
New Haven, CT 06515
www.ibsassociation.org

National Digestive Diseases Information Clearinghouse
2 Information Way
Bethesda, MD 20892-3570
tel: (800) 891-5389
www.digestive.niddk.nih.gov

National Heart, Lung, and Blood Institute
P.O. Box 30105
Bethesda, MD 20824-0105
tel: (301) 592 8573
www.nhlbi.nih.gov

National Osteoporosis Foundation
1232 22nd Street N.W.
Washington, D.C. 20037-1292
tel: (202) 223-2226
www.nof.org

Nutrition.gov
www.nutrition.gov

Organic Consumers Association
6101 Cliff Estate Road
Little Marais, MN 55614
tel: (218) 226-4164
www.organicconsumers.org

ORGANIZATIONS IN CANADA

Canadian Celiac Association
5170 Dixie Road, Suite 204
Mississauga, ON L4W 1E3
tel: (800) 363-7296
www.celiac.ca

Canadian Diabetes
Association
15 Toronto St.
Suite 800
Toronto, ON M5C 2E3
tel: (800) BANTING
www.diabetes.ca

Canadian Organic Growers
125 South Knowlesville Road
Knowlesville, NB E7L 1B1
tel: (506) 375-7383
www.cog.ca

The Canadian Society of Allergy
and Clinical Immunology
774 Echo Dr.
Ottawa ON K1S 5N8
tel: (613) 730-6272
www.csaci.medical.org

Crohn's and Colitis Foundation
of Canada
60 St. Clair Avenue East,
Suite 600
Toronto, ON M4T 1N5
tel: (800) 387-1479
www.ccfc.ca

Dietitians of Canada
480 University Avenue, Suite 604
Toronto, ON M5G 1V2
tel: 416-596-0857
www.dietitians.ca

Heart and Stroke Foundation
of Canada
222 Queen Street
Suite 1402
Ottawa, ON K1P 5V9
tel: (613) 569-4361
www.heartandstroke.ca

Irritable Bowel Syndrome
Association
P.O. Box 94074
Toronto, ON M4N 3R1
www.ibsassociation.ca

National Institute of
Nutrition
408 Queen Street, 3rd Floor
Ottawa, ON K1R 5A7
tel: (613) 235-3355
www.nin.ca

Osteoporosis Society of
Canada
33 Laird Drive
Toronto, ON M4G 3S9
Tel: (800) 463-6842
www.osteoporosis.ca

Index

Page numbers in *italics* indicate recipes.

About the author

Ian Marber
Nutrition consultant, author,
television and health journalist

Ian studied at London's renowned Institute for Optimum Nutrition, and now heads the Food Doctor clinic at Notting Hill, London. He contributes regularly to many of Britain's leading magazines and newspapers, and is a sought-after guest on both television and radio.

Undiagnosed food sensitivities in his twenties led to Ian becoming interested in nutrition. His condition was later identified as celiac disease, an intolerance to gluten. He is now an acknowledged expert on nutrition and digestion, and many of his clients are referred to the Food Doctor clinic by doctors and gastroenterologists.

Ian advises on all aspects of nutrition, and in particular on the impact that correct food choices can have on an individual's health and weight. He is known by his clients to give highly motivational, positive and practical advice that can make a real difference to their well-being.

His first book *The Food Doctor,* was cowritten with Vicki Edgson, in September 1999. To date, this title has sold over 300,000 copies and has been translated into nine languages, including French, Spanish, and Swedish. Ian's first solo title, *The Food Doctor in the City,* published in 2000, highlighted how to stay healthy in an urban environment. It has sold well worldwide, notably in Australia and the Far East. In September 2001 he released *In Bed with The Food Doctor,* which examines how nutriton can improve your libido and help you sleep well.

About the Food Doctor

Ian Marber and Vicki Edgson cofounded their Food Doctor nutrition practice in 1999 following the success of their original book, *The Food Doctor—Healing Foods for Mind and Body.* The consultancy is now a leading provider of nutritional information and services, including a busy clinic in London with a network of nutrition consultants. The Food Doctor offers one-on-one consultations, workshops, and lectures on a wide variety of subjects such as weight loss, children's nutrition, digestive health, and stress management. It also works with major corporate clients to improve the health and well-being of their employees and frequently advises catering companies on their menus.

Acknowledgments

The author would like to thank:
Dame Shirley Bassey, Yvonne Bishop, Marylisa Browne, Simon Carey, Liz Claridge, Michael da Costa, Diane Filipovski, Stephen Garrett, Rebecca Haywood, Lisa Howells, Jani Isaacs, Shannon Leeman, Emma Lo, David Manning, Susie Perry, Rita Rakus, Stuart Scher, Antonia Smith, Robert Shrager, Mary Thomas, and, of course, my family.

Special thanks to Rowena Paxton for her delicious recipes, and to her family for being willing guinea pigs; to MC for her support and trust; and to the lovely Susannah Steel for her wonderful work in editing this book, and for making me laugh during stressful times.

The publisher would like to thank:
Penny Warren, Shannon Beatty, and Julia Roles for editorial assistance and Sarah Rock for design assistance.